Reconstructing Mabel
A Taos Memoir

Reconstructing Mabel

A Taos Memoir

VALMAI
HOWE
ELKINS

SUNSTONE PRESS
SANTA FE

© 2019 by Valmai Howe Elkins
All Rights Reserved
No part of this book may be reproduced in any form or by any electronic or mechanical means including
information storage and retrieval systems without permission in writing from the publisher, except by a reviewer who may quote brief passages in a review.

Sunstone books may be purchased for educational, business, or sales promotional use. For information please write: Special Markets Department, Sunstone Press, P.O. Box 2321, Santa Fe, New Mexico 87504-2321.

Book and cover design › L.R. Ahl
Printed on acid-free paper
∞

Library of Congress Cataloging-in-Publication Data

Names: Elkins, Valmai Howe, author.
Title: Reconstructing Mabel : a Taos memoir / by Valmai Howe Elkins.
Description: Santa Fe : Sunstone Press, [2019] | Includes bibliographical references.
Identifiers: LCCN 2019002025 | ISBN 9781632932587 (pbk. : alk. paper)
Subjects: LCSH: Elkins, Valmai Howe. | Luhan, Mabel Dodge, 1879-1962--Homes and haunts--New Mexico--Taos. | Taos (N.M.)--Biography. | Intellectuals--New Mexico--Taos--Biography.
Classification: LCC F804.T2 E44 2019 | DDC 978.9/53--dc23
LC record available at https://lccn.loc.gov/2019002025

WWW.SUNSTONEPRESS.COM
SUNSTONE PRESS / POST OFFICE BOX 2321 / SANTA FE, NM 87504-2321 /USA
(505) 988-4418 / ORDERS ONLY (800) 243-5644 / FAX (505) 988-1025

Dedication

For Susan Bossenberry, Carolynn Rafman, Susanna Tvede, and for Mabel's Girls

Contents

Preface ~ 9
Acknowledgments ~ 12

Two Arrivals: 1917 and 1991 ~ 15
The Big House at the End of the Lane ~ 20
A Terrible Mistake? ~ 21
Roosevelt's Signature ~ 25
Mabel the Writer ~ 28
A Woman's War ~ 30
Writing in the Hills: Bennington College ~ 32
Winter in Bennington ~ 35
Homesteading ~ 37
The Art of Living Alone ~ 39
Mabel: The Facts ~ 40
A Bridge Between Two Cultures ~ 50
At the Taos Book Shop ~52
Susanna's Mother: The Taos Society of Artists ~ 54
At the Pueblo ~ 58
Doing Nothing ~ 60
At The Pinch Penny Wash 'O' Mat: The Other Taos ~ 64
The Forbidden Paintings ~ 67
Becoming Local ~ 69
The House Next Door ~ 71
The Count ~ 76
Summer of 1929 ~ 79
The Lawrence Women ~ 80
Remembering Mabel: Lunch with Phoebe Cottam ~ 88
Tea At Phoebe's ~ 96
Caffé Tazza ~ 97
Calling All Angels ~ 99

The End of the Universe Café: Salted Peanuts ~ 102
The Taos Hum ~ 104
Homage to Mabel: The Salon ~ 106
Mabel's Pooch: Rescuing Aslan ~ 110
The Darker Side ~ 120
Mabel's Secret ~ 133
A Passion for Houses ~ 138
Building Mabel's Home ~ 141
A Bowl of Lemons ~ 142
The Hospital Birthing Room ~ 145
The Birth of Mabel's Son ~ 147
Mabel's Rooms ~ 152
House Whispering ~ 155
The House: Sanctuary or Prison? ~ 158
Mabel: Privileged or Deprived? ~ 160
Mabel and Tony ~ 164
Mabel At Home ~ 166
Mabel's Girls: Free To Create ~ 168
Mabel's Girls: A Safe Place ~ 172
Mabel's Girls: A Place To Meet Yourself ~ 175
Painting Intuitively ~ 177
Christmas Eve at the Pueblo ~ 180
Santa Fe ~ 182
Return To Taos ~ 185
Mabel's Grave ~ 190

Epilogue ~ 192
Bibliography ~ 194
Notes ~ 196

Preface

I arrived in Taos, New Mexico in January, 1991. Alone and timid, I was escaping the severe east coast winter and my increasingly severe bouts of bronchitis. The small adobe house and studio on Morada Lane had been built, according to a deed signed by Franklin D. Roosevelt, by Mabel Dodge Luhan and her husband Tony. Later, when I met Natalie Goldberg, author of *Writing Down the Bones,* she told me, "You're living in the right house. We held the first women's writing workshop there on June 12, 1973."

"Mabel was a wealthy socialite and patron of the arts," the realtor told me. "She and her fourth husband, Tony Luhan from the Taos Pueblo, built the big house up from you and she invited D. H. Lawrence and Georgia O'Keeffe and dozens of other writers and artists to stay. Now it's a B&B and they run all sorts of personal growth workshops."

For the next twelve winters I walked up the hill to Mabel's each morning where I thrived on the warm and friendly welcomes. Her quirky house intrigued me. The rambling adobe with softly curving rooms, artfully piled, was topped by Mabel's bedroom with windows facing the sacred mountain of the Pueblo. Beyond the house stretched miles of Pueblo sage plains and a large white wooden cross, painted by O'Keeffe as *Black Cross.*

Mabel, born in Buffalo, New York in 1879, had presided over salons in New York and Florence, and drawn together some of the most influential writers of the early twentieth century, but I was most interested in her own writing. Her two books, *Edge of Taos Desert* and *Winter in Taos,* she wrote with refreshing candor and sensitivity to the land and its people. She and the home she'd loved inspired my own work.

I have written this book to weave the life of Mabel in Taos with my own experiences and those of other contemporary women influenced by her life and writings. She wrote about the details of daily life managing the Big House. I describe my own modest attempts at homesteading. She wrote about the dogs she rescued. I write about the dramatic rescue of Aslan, my Russian wolfhound. She described her salons and lavish parties. I describe the salon my friends and I held in my living room, so tiny it could only hold six, about the fun we had and the meals we enjoyed together. She explored the shadow side of her life. I try to do the same with my own.

Mabel wrote volumes of memoir. I had four books published when I arrived in Taos; two works of non-fiction and two novels. My Taos winters yielded two more books.

One evening at a party, my friend and neighbor, Susan Bossenberry, came up to me. "I want to introduce you to Phoebe Cottam. Her mother was a good friend of Mabel's and when Phoebe married and was starting a family, Mabel offered the Big House to her. Mabel and Tony were getting on and they'd moved to a smaller house across the road. Phoebe has all sorts of great stories about them. Maybe you could write about her."

Phoebe and I met for lunch at the Taos Inn, then once again at her home. She brought to life Mabel and her two friends, Frieda Lawrence and artist, Dorothy Brett. "They all doted on my son, John Brooke and he would sit on Mabel's lap while we drank bourbon and one day he became rambunctious and Brett said, "I hope you're not giving that baby anything to drink, Mabel."

Over the next twelve winters I gradually came to know contemporary women who had attended the programs at Mabel's. My friend and poet, Carolynn Rafman, who spent summers at Mabel's told me, "There's a bunch of us who've been inspired by Mabel and her house. She's helped us change our lives. We call ourselves Mabel's Girls. Every year we take a photo of ourselves on the staircase to Mabel's bedroom and on her bed." Intrigued, I set out to talk with some of these women.

My arrival at Mabel's little house was a pivotal point in my life. At the peak of my career, I felt worn down by chronic ill-health and initially, viewed my time in Taos more as exile than opportunity. Mabel helped restore my confidence. Until her death in 1962, she lived a bold and uncompromising life, taking whatever risks necessary to be true to herself. I have tried to do the same.

The year 2017 marked the centennial of Mabel's arrival in Taos. The film, *Awakening In Taos* and the gallery exhibit, *Mabel Dodge Luhan and Company* have triggered renewed interest in her remarkable life and influence.

I am grateful to Mabel, and to my friend Susan for insisting I write this book, and for introducing me to Phoebe Cottam, who passed, August 18, 2017. I am also most grateful to the women at Mabel's who welcomed me and to those who shared their experiences and stories. It is my hope that you are also inspired by their bold spirits.

Acknowledgments

As always, the first people to thank are David, my husband and Tilke, my daughter, endlessly wise and supportive, who have encouraged me to leap into the unknown, and who are not afraid to head out themselves along the road less traveled. From the moment they first visited me in New Mexico escaping those damp eastern winters, they have been eager to listen to the details of this project. Thank you Tilke, for your help with final copy editing.

Thank you friend and good neighbor, Susan Bossenberry for our laughs and escapades with our borzoi, for introducing me to Phoebe Cottam and insisting I write this book. To Susanna Tvede, my first friend in Taos, you continue to encourage my writing, celebrate the Southwest and reminisce about our Taos days. I am so grateful for the photos of your mother in Taos in 1924 and you at the Taos Book Shop, 1992.

Thank you dear Maria Fortin for welcoming me with radiant kindness all those winter mornings when I trooped up the hill to Mabel's.

Thank you my longtime friend Carolynn Rafman, for sharing experiences at Mabel's, delighting me with tales of Mabel's Girls and rallying the Girls for photographs.

Thank you Judy Jordan for sharing your time at Mabel's, thank you Katrin Themlitz for describing feelings and insights during the Intuitive Painting program at Mabel's.

Thank you, delightful new friends, Selina Appleby and Elsie Lailey for taking the time to read the final manuscript with enthusiasm and insight.

I have such happy memories of vivacious, generous Phoebe Cottam, one of the Great Ladies of Taos. I am so grateful for the fun we shared over delicious meals as she entertained me with vivid memories of Mabel and Friends.

A special thank you to James Clois Smith, Jr. I was delighted when my quest for an attentive, encouraging publisher led me past the O'Keeffe Museum on Johnson Street and into the welcoming home of Sunstone Press.

Two Arrivals: 1917 and 1991

In 1917, thirty-eight-year old Mabel Ganson Evans Dodge Sterne left her New York apartment at 23 Fifth Avenue, to visit the Southwest. Her sculptor husband, Maurice Sterne, had gone on ahead. He urged her, for the good of her health, to take the train out to Santa Fe and meet him.

"I had always heard of people going to Florida or California, and more occasionally to the West, but no one ever went to the Southwest. Hardly anyone had ever heard of Santa Fe."[1] She set off for "perhaps a fortnight." Two weeks after her arrival she made the journey to Taos.

"My life broke in two right then, and I entered into the second half, a new world that replaced all the ways I had known with others, more strange and terrible and sweet than any I had ever been able to imagine."[2]

At four in the afternoon, January 11, 1991, my four wheel drive pushed through deep snow into the parking area of 220 Morada Lane, Taos. Beyond the Mabel Dodge Luhan House, at 240, the sacred mountain rose from the sage plain of the pueblo against a darkening sky, but the sheet of blowing snow obliterated the view.

My traveling companions, Bianca the eight-year-old Russian wolfhound, and my friend Meredith's eighteen year old son, Adam, slogged with me through the snowy garden. When we unlocked the front door, the tiny house felt cold and unwelcoming. Had I made a terrible mistake?

If I'd thought at all about the Southwest, I envisioned a dry wind blowing across a desert dotted here and there with dusty mud huts. Perhaps a couple of Georgia O'Keeffe's sun bleached skulls. I had never heard of Mabel Dodge Luhan.

Then in the summer of 1990, my friend Meredith Webster, learned of an intriguing project in southern Colorado. Canadian businessman, Maurice Strong and his Danish-born wife, Hanne, had bought a vast tract of wilderness in the St. Luis Valley to create their vision of a global village for spiritual leaders and environmentalists, a place where political and business leaders could come to be taught how to care for themselves and the Earth. When Meredith invited our friend, Cynthia Drummond and me to accompany her, the timing seemed perfect.

Six months earlier, after a bout of bronchitis followed by pneumonia, my doctor had told me, "You've been sick every winter now for years. You've got to get away. Somewhere dry. The Southwest would be ideal. You could teach your Fall course at McGill and leave before it gets too cold. Why not do your writing down there for the winter?"

"I can't leave my husband, he has his business here."

My doctor's kind face turned stern. "If you don't get away soon you'll be leaving your husband permanently."

Meredith, Cynthia and I flew south from Denver to Alamosa in a small plane and drove to the tiny hamlet of Crestone at 7,800 feet. The Baca ranch, set at the western base of the Sangre de Christo mountains which tower up to 14,000 feet, was a pristine wilderness of shade trees, forests, meadows and clear streams, the buildings designed to blend with the surrounds. We would learn that it was home to more than seventy species of rare plants and animals.

The land had been dubbed simply "The Baca" after a Spanish land-grant to the Baca family. At the time of our visit, the Strongs had already given hundreds of acres to Carmelite Catholics, Tibetan Buddhist monks, Zen monks, indigenous tribes and the Sri Aurobindo Learning Center. They planned a seed bank for crops viable at high altitudes, a world nutrition center and various healing centers. Hanne showed us the small Carmelite monastery already built, blending perfectly into the landscape and we visited a Tibetan *stupa* underway.

Indigenous people in the area had long believed that the land was a place of extraordinary natural power, a place where peoples from many tribes could come together for ceremony. Fittingly, our visit coincided with a moonlit evening of tribal dances and drumming.

After the ceremonies, I was studying a map of the Southwest. For years I'd enjoyed writing the occasional travel piece, and now two exciting stories were within easy reach. Mission Wolf, a sanctuary for discarded pet wolves caught my interest, just a short drive from the Baca Ranch. As I studied the map further, I noticed also that Abiquii, New Mexico, was only 121 miles. This seemed an ideal time to finally visit Ghost Ranch and the land which had inspired Georgia O'Keeffe's bright, bold paintings.

I set off early next morning in a rental car. That night at Mission Wolf the unearthly singing of the wolves in their enclosures just outside my tipi enthralled me in the hours before a spectacular sunrise.

After breakfast, I followed a two lane highway which curved south at the base of the mountains, onto quiet back roads lined with small western sunflowers, purple daisies and bright coral Indian paintbrush. Plains of sage replaced fields. A brilliant sun beat down. The country looked somehow familiar. Later I would piece together memories of the seventies movie, *Easy Rider,* where motorcycle scenes with Dennis Hopper, Peter Fonda and Jack Nicholson had been filmed along this road.

A sign announced the mountain town of Taos. On the left stretched flat pasture dotted with lean cows and rough-coated horses. Beyond, rose a spectacular mountain. Tourists crept south, bumper to bumper along the single road into town, the Paseo del Norte. A jumble of low brown art galleries and gift stores trimmed in bright blue and turquoise lined the way. Bunches of red chili peppers hung by the doorways and voluptuous pink hollyhocks, bright orange California poppies and deep blue cornflowers jostled along the paths. The place felt exuberant. Instead of my initial plan to drive straight through to Abiquiu for the

O'Keeffe research, I made a quick decision to spend the night in Taos.

Casa Feliz, an old adobe on Bent Street, turned Bed and Breakfast, conveniently had a room. I managed to complete the trip to Abiquiu, visit Ghost Ranch and O'Keeffe's house in the village and return to Taos in time for a late dinner and a tankard of mead at The Apple Tree, just a few doors from Casa Feliz.

Next morning I woke eager to explore this quirky little town. The historic plaza was a short stroll down Bent Street and through the John Dunn Plaza. A woman with a rag mop was cleaning the worn wooden floor of the five and dime and the store smelled of Murphy's Oil. With a fresh notebook and a latte from World Coffee, where a group of motorcycles was already parked, I was returning to Casa Feliz when a woman popped out from behind a fence. She was friendly.

"What do you do?" she asked.

"I'm a writer."

"Boy, do I have the perfect writing studio for you! Hop in my car and I'll show you."

I noticed the Real Estate office at the end of her path. Perhaps it was the thrum of the motor cycles. I was ready for adventure.

We turned left from the main street onto Kit Carson, where galleries lined the covered boardwalk, then made another quick turn left, beside the blue trimmed Casa Benavides Inn. Quickly the paving narrowed to a dusty lane. The realtor pulled into a parking area in front of a high *latilla* fence. I followed her as she unlocked a gate. At the top of four stone steps was a pretty garden. There was something storybookish about the way the morning sunlight filtered through the leaves of a twisted old apple tree.

"I can't show you inside because the owner's away, and I have to give her twenty four hours notice, but we can peep through the door," said the realtor.

There were two buildings; a tiny house with a quaint wood and glass wrap-around greenhouse filled with unusually large red geraniums, and across a brick patio, a small studio with a wall of glass overlooking the apple tree. When I peered in the front door of the house, I saw the rich dark wood of aged floors, the hulk of an antique cook stove, low dark beams and a world of potential.

I stood beside that twisted old tree. Bees buzzed around fallen apples. A long tailed magpie flew onto the patch of grass and warbled at us. The light in the leaves was the color of honey.

"I'll take it."

The realtor looked as stunned as I felt.

I was due back in Denver that afternoon to rejoin my friends for the flight to Montreal. There was no way I could examine the house. We returned to the realty office and I made my offer.

"I think I've bought a writing studio in Taos." I told my husband by phone.

After a brief silence he said. "That's wonderful. When can I see it?"

"I'm closing in November, but the realtor says the owner wants to stay 'til January, so she'd rent it back. You could come for Easter."

The Big House at the End of the Lane

The realtor had driven me up a short hill to the end of the dusty lane and pointed through a pair of massive wooden gates set in a high adobe wall. Around a flagstoned courtyard lined with tall dovecotes, rose a large rambling adobe with uneven, rounded corners. On the second floor, a room full of windows painted with whimsical designs opened to a covered portal. Perched atop the house, another room of windows overlooked that extraordinary mountain. It reminded me of the houses I used to make with my set of wooden blocks, topped with a pirate lookout.

Later, when I visited the Taos Pueblo, the connection between that pyramid of mud cubes and the house at the end of the lane would be clear.

"That's the Mabel Dodge Luhan House," said the realtor. I looked blank. "She was a wealthy socialite from Buffalo. She visited Taos with her third husband in 1917 and she fell in love with Tony Luhan from the Taos Pueblo. He became her fourth husband and they built this house, then she invited all these artists and writers to visit; Georgia O'Keeffe and D. H. Lawrence and Ansel Adams. Your little house was one of her guest houses. Somebody told me Carl Jung stayed there." She paused, then added, "There's actually a framed copy just inside the front door of a deed signed by President Roosevelt granting the land to Tony and Mabel."

A Terrible Mistake?

"We reached the high desert of Taos Valley at twilight and saw the sacred mountain, twenty miles away, standing out in bright distinctness, lighted by a sun that had already sunk below the horizon. The snow patches on the three peaks of the bow-shaped crest were transparently pink, and all the deep flanks of the southern slopes were purple plum color. The low light of dusk made the shapes like pyramids stand out so clearly the range seemed made up of cones, piled one upon the other. Very huge and splendid it was."
—Mabel Dodge Luhan. *Edge of Taos Desert*.

That late afternoon of January 11, 1991, 220 Morada Lane was no longer the gently seductive sunny place I'd bought in November and leased back to the owner until I could leave Montreal. The old apple tree I'd fallen in love with slumped forwards, heavy with snow, and the tiny adobe house seemed a cheerless hovel. Naked bulbs hung from their cords and the antique wood stove I'd admired was choked with old ashes. Not a stick of wood to be seen. There wasn't even a piece of toilet paper. Fortunately when we cranked up the noisy gas heater the house began to warm.

"Wouldn't it be nice if we were coming somewhere furnished, with a TV." said Adam wistfully as he surveyed the bleak rooms. He was exhausted from driving three hours in the blizzard from The San Jon Motel near the New Mexico border, where my first tumbleweed had rolled along the front porch beside the pay phone. We'd stopped for coffee at Wild Oats in Santa Fe. Then while Adam slept, I drove the final stretch, creeping around the bends of the Rio Grande gorge. Once when the visibility was so bad I could scarcely see the white line, I felt a comforting touch on my knee. Bianca, standing on the back seat, had reached across with her long white paw. Two hours later we emerged from the last twist of a road now treacherous with snow and ice.

The house was unfurnished except for a small oak table and chairs and two uninviting mattresses on the floor, one in a room which just managed to hold the mattress, the other in a larger room where the pattern on the linoleum was worn thin.

"It would be nice," I said to Adam. "But that wouldn't be the pioneering spirit of the Southwest, would it?"

I said to myself, I think I've made a terrible mistake. Whatever had possessed me to buy a house sight unseen? Had all those years of bronchitis unhinged my mind? Why hadn't I just rented a comfortable modern condo for the winter? Maybe I should have stayed put in Montreal under the bluish light of the full-spectrum lamp for Seasonal Affective Disorder and taken a chance with my health. I lay in my sleeping bag on the forlorn mattress, close to tears. I missed my husband. I wanted to go home.

My first morning in Taos, while Adam was still sleeping, I stepped out into the garden with Bianca. The air was crisp and sun sparkled on the fresh snow. My long-legged white borzoi pranced beside me as I trudged up the small hill towards Mabel's. Bluish smoke rose from the Big House, rich with an unfamiliar fragrance I learned was the *piñon* wood used in all the fireplaces. Somewhere the sound of an axe rang out. The sky was an unfamiliar shade of rich mauvish blue, a shade described in paint catalogues as "antique lavender."

Bianca and I paused outside the high adobe wall of Mabel's. The massive carved wooden gates stood open beneath an aged bell hung from an adobe arch. As we stepped into the rough-paved courtyard bordered along one side by a covered walkway, the *portal*, a cloud of pigeons rose into the frozen air from a row of high dovecotes. I noticed the colorful porcelain roosters along the roof line. Beyond the courtyard the sun caught a row of lacy cottonwood trees, which lined a small creek bed, an *acequia,* now dry. A few golden leaves still clung to the branches. The house looked inviting. I looped Bianca's long leash around a tree near the gates. "I'll be back soon." She was used to waiting.

The front door was unlocked. The living room smelled of wood smoke and comfort and a fire crackled in a fireplace made from the same adobe as the walls. The ceiling was distinctive; thin sticks arranged herringbone style and stained a washed out rainbow of colors. The furniture was the kind you sink into. Well-stuffed bookcases lined the walls. The light was muted and restful.

The house appeared deserted, so I followed the smell of fresh coffee and stepped down into a large dining room, the floor tiled in black and reddish-brown squares. Sturdy oak tables were set for breakfast. Somewhere behind the room a pot clanged. A woman with friendly dark eyes stepped out from a kitchen at the back and greeted me.

"I've just moved into two-twenty Morada Lane," I told her, "and it's pretty bleak down there."

The woman, whose name was Maria, smiled a wonderful welcoming smile. It turned out that Mabel's was now home to Las Palomas, a bed and breakfast and cultural center offering workshops which explored mind-body integration, creativity and consciousness. Though an occasional man attended, in the winters which followed, I'd see mostly women walking down the hill past my little house, sometimes in small groups, but often alone with notebooks in hand. Later, I would learn about "Mabel's Girls."

"We've got a group in for Natalie Goldberg's writing workshop," Maria told me, "so there's lots going on right now, but any time you're feeling lonely just come on up."

I did. For the next twelve winters Maria Fortin welcomed me warmly and Mabel's became my anchor as I absorbed an extraordinary new life, one free from the bronchitis which had stalked me since childhood.

I finally met Natalie Goldberg, author of the hugely popular *Writing Down the Bones.* I told her I lived down the lane. When she discovered it was at 220, she seemed very pleased. "You live at the right house," she said. "On June twelfth, nineteen seventy-three, we held the first women's writing workshop in America. The house was owned by Rosemary back then."

Only a barbed wire fence and a rough gate that leaned crookedly to the ground, separated Mabel's house from a vast stretch of sage-covered plain rising to that majestic mountain. I took my time absorbing the view while Bianca explored the new smells.

Mabel's house fascinated me. What sort of person would build a place which, long after her death, would continue to attract and welcome so many creative energies? When I began to read Mabel's memoirs, the first thing that struck me was her deep feeling for the land itself. On one occasion, out with Tony, she simply wanted to lie face down on the ground and feel the powerful earth energies. Not exactly what I would associate with a person the realtor had described as a "wealthy socialite."

I would agree with Mabel that the mountain felt a living breathing presence, complete in itself. Each morning I'd stand at the edge of the Pueblo desert, inhale the pungence of sage and gaze at what I came to think of as "my mountain."

In the sunshine of that first morning my little studio felt less grim. "What it needs is whitewash," I told Adam as he prepared to walk down the lane to The Taos Inn, which ran a bus to the Ski Valley. He looked dubious.

I drove the few minutes to Randall's Lumber, the sort of old-fashioned store soon to be threatened by what some locals referred to as "the outside world." The store smelled of wood floors, turpentine and laundry detergent. When I selected two huge buckets of white paint and all the accompanying paraphernalia, together with a tea kettle, the white-haired man at the desk took his time and made sure I left with my bill hand written on a piece of yellow paper with a carbon copy. I drove to the pick-up door where a guy with a long grey ponytail hoisted the cans into the trunk.

Roosevelt's Signature

When I returned to 220 Morada Lane, I filled my new yellow tea kettle and lit the gas stove for a cup of tea. Then I unpacked the box of china, the cups and plates with the cheerful blue and white roosters I'd brought from Montreal. While the water heated I peered at the framed certificate the realtor had mentioned, hanging on the wall beside the stove.

The opening paragraph described the parcel of land on which the house was built, containing eight acres and seven hundred forty-eight thousands of an acre, according to the approved Plat of Survey of said Land on file in the General Land Office. The following paragraph was more interesting:

> *Now Know Ye, that the United States of America, in consideration of the premises, and in conformity with the provisions of the act aforesaid, HAS GIVEN AND GRANTED, and by these presents DOES GIVE AND GRANT, unto the said Manuel de Jesus Trujillo and Mabel Lujan, and to their heirs, the Land above described; to HAVE AND TO HOLD the same unto the said Manuel de Jesus Trujillo and Mabel Lujan, and to their heirs and assigns forever; with the proviso in said Act expressed that this patent shall have the effect only of a relinquishment by the United States of America and the Indians of said Pueblo. In testimony whereof, I, Franklin D. Roosevelt, President of the United States of America, have caused these letters to be*

made Patent, and the seal of the General and Office to be hereunto affixed. Given under my hand, at the City of Washington, the twenty-ninth day of August, in the year of the Lord one thousand nine hundred and thirty-four and of the Independence of the United States the one hundred and fifty ninth.

This was followed by Roosevelt's signature. Was Manuel de Jesus Trujillo the legal name of Mabel's Pueblo husband, Tony Luhan? I liked the idea that this tiny adobe studio, bought on a whim, was connected to that fairytale house at the top of the lane.

I turned off the gas, removed the whistling kettle and poured a pot of Earl Grey tea, which I carried to the round oak table. Across from the table, a pair of narrow, obviously hand-made glass doors, opened into the narrow little greenhouse. I liked the way the sunlight caught the vibrant red geraniums. Instead of the pots I'd assumed contained them, they were growing in a wide indoor bed of earth, set in the uneven stone floor. The sunlight also caught the masses of cobwebs woven around the beams.

For the first time since the four day drive from Montreal, I had a chance to just sit. Bianca was stretched on my mattress, fast asleep after the morning's walk. What had I done? Suddenly this old adobe house, the snowy garden, the shimmering sunlight and the strange alluring house at the top of the lane felt not quite real.

As I sipped my tea in the tiny low-beamed room with the refrigerator humming along with the buzz of the gas heater, I suddenly felt exhausted and a jumble of anxieties surfaced. Was I really ready for this health-imposed exile? For the first time, I had arranged a winter away from the work which had absorbed me since I graduated. I'd taught childbirth education at a women's hospital, then, while teaching at McGill University, introduced the concept of a hospital birthing room. Since then I'd combined teaching with traveling to hospitals as a birthing room consultant.

The idea of just lying around and admiring the scenery felt like dropping out. "Think of all the time you'll have for your writing," my friends, Meredith and Cynthia, had tried to reassure me. I had some tentative plans for a new book but right now this felt overwhelming. I'd always fitted my writing around my full time work. In this new, strange solitude, cut free from any familiar schedules, there would be no excuse if I didn't pursue my passion and produce another novel.

I didn't feel like writing. Instead, I browsed the bookshelves in the office up at Mabel's and bought both volumes of her Taos memoirs. Her voice in *Edge of Taos Desert,* and *Winter in Taos*, I found intimate and compelling. These two books quickly drew me into the luminous world she and her husband, Tony, had created at the top of Morada Lane.

Mabel the Writer

After I finished reading *Edge of Taos Desert*, I would learn that Mabel had begun to take her writing seriously, urged on by A. A. Brill, leader of the psychoanalytic movement in America, as a way to overcome what she described as her recurrent "melancholy." In 1913, she had written an article which appeared in *Arts and Decorations*, about Gertrude Stein, who had written a short piece, *Portrait of Mabel Dodge*. Mabel wrote that Stein was doing with words what Picasso was doing with paint. "She is impelling language to induce new states of consciousness, and in doing so, language becomes with her a creative art, rather than a mirror of history."[3]

The International Show of Modern Art was in its planning stages and thousands of copies of her article on Stein were sold. Stein's *Portrait of Mabel Dodge*, followed by the piece in *Arts and Decorations*, did much to put Mabel out there as a writer whose ideas were worth reading.

Later, when Mabel visited Brill from her country retreat, where she was enjoying some respite from the dirt and noise of New York City, he did his best to convince her that she'd be "more at home in some skyscraper, with telephones, push buttons and alert secretaries to carry out my plans than among the Sweet Williams and pheasants of Finney Farm."[4]

To pacify Brill, she called her friend, Arthur Brisbane, who for the past fifteen years had been trying to convince her that she was a writer.

When she suggested she write for his *New York Journal*, he offered her a biweekly column. She could write the column in about an hour, sitting on her bed at Finney Farm. Her articles were syndicated by the Hearst Corporation to every newspaper in the US and the editors promoted articles such as "Mabel Dodge Writes About Mother Love" and "Mabel Dodge Asks Do You Work For A Living?" Mabel found her new identity embarrassing as "Mabel Dodge" entered the circle of "Dorothy Dix" and suchlike.

Her new writing activity, did however, appear to placate Brill. Her articles later expanded to include her knowledge and experience of the new psychoanalysis.

A Woman's War

As the weather in New York grew warm, Mabel left for Provincetown where her writer friends, Neith and Hopkins Hapgood summered among the "double line of small white clapboard cottages along a silent village street, between the bay and the open sea."[5] Plays written by the Hapgoods and others who formed The Provincetown Players, absorbed and entertained the tiny community.

Mabel and Neith took a ship to Florence with Boyce, the oldest Hapgood boy and best friend of Mabel's son, John, and three year-old Beatrix Hapgood. Shortly after their arrival in 1914, war was declared. Amidst the frenzy which ensued, Mabel said that war didn't interest or excite her. She wrote, "All the other American journalists were already in Paris and everybody was excited, pleased, happy. Everybody but me, I thought."[6]

Later, she produced for the publication, *The Masses*, a serious and important anti-war piece, called *The Secret of War*, subtitled "*The Look on the Faces of Men who have been Killing—and what Women Think about it*."

She interviewed wounded soldiers and their wives and concluded, "To maintain the illusion of Empire, women are urging their men into the field...fathers are sending their sons up to the last." Her penetrating conclusion that "The only hope of permanent peace lies in a woman's war against war"[7] may arguably be most relevant today, one hundred years since she wrote the article.

After she made her home in Taos, she continued to develop the one area of her life not dependent on the vagaries of relationships or health: her writing. For the next decade she would embark on the four-volume *Intimate Memories*, which detailed her life from birth up to, and including her time in Taos.

According to her long time friend, Dorothy Brett, Mabel was extraordinarily disciplined, reclining on a chaise for hours at a time with notebook and pencil.

Writing in the Hills: Bennington College

An avid reader from early childhood on, Mabel wrote, "Books sent my clamorous spirit into another world."

I emphatically agreed. My own journey into the glorious escape of storytelling began on my maternal grandmother's lap. "Tell me a story about a naughty little girl," I would coax. She was happy to oblige and her source of material proved a bottomless pit.

At age four my father presented me with a tiny notebook filled with blank pages. He sharpened my black lead pencils to a pleasing point and I announced that I would write a story. Like my heroine, Enid Blyton, I wanted to write stories of mystery and adventure. And I did, piling up my little notebooks. But somehow, as I grew older, I limited myself to meticulous journaling. By the time I left home, my fiction had dried up as I plunged into my career.

In my twenties and early thirties, I'd written a series of travel pieces and had two non-fiction books published. Based on my work in childbirth education, *The Rights of the Pregnant Parent*, had done well, been translated and printed in multiple editions. Later it would be hailed as "The book that changed hospital birth." I was grateful that my writing could help change the status quo, but my dream was to write a novel.

Then one Montreal Sunday morning at the breakfast table, my husband, David, was leafing through *Esquire*. "Here's something for you. It's called *Writing in the Hills*," he said. "*Get drunk, get laid, get published*," he read, and added, "Forget the first two. Here's your chance."

Bennington College in summer is a southern Vermont paradise

of rolling green hills, wildflowers and long, firefly-studded evenings. I dipped my toe in the water with a summer Writers' Workshop. After coming of age in the old-style educational system which discouraged any flutter of individuality, together with the slightest expression of feelings, my time at Bennington felt like a sudden release from suffocating darkness into light. Here was a place which actually celebrated individual creativity and encouraged us to mine the depths of our emotional history.

My fellow students and I formed a tight little group which helped me overcome a deep-seated fear of writing fiction. The following year I applied for the Master of Fine Arts program, which conveniently combined on-location with correspondence, allowing me to integrate it with my work schedule.

I was already struggling to free myself from the block that limited my writing, which at Bennington I discovered was a fear of exposing emotions. I had been raised "stiff upper lip," to be exquisitely polite, and never show any messy feelings. While this might contribute to a civilized dinner party, it is counterproductive when you're writing fiction.

The MFA in creative writing was serious stuff. In order to graduate, each of us had to write a work of "publishable quality." Holed up in my room in one of the white clapboard student houses, I finally immersed myself in a novel, a world of struggling for the authentic.

The clacking and buzzing of word processors and printers from each of the rooms along the hall felt encouraging. At mealtimes we talked earnestly about our work and gossiped about our professors, Richard Elman and Nicholas Delbanco.

Richard, held in high esteem for his screenplay of *Taxi Driver,* could be terrifying. With his big booming voice, he exposed the flaws in our efforts in a way that made us cringe, then do better. Later, we discovered the kindness and devotion beneath his tough words.

Nicholas was the esteemed author of the *Sherbrookes* trilogy. His style of criticism could best be described as iron hand under the velvet glove, no less effective. Our first morning he told us, "If you want to be a writer you have to get used to Rejection. Rejection one, rejection two, and then some."

They were an impressive duo and like skilled potters they coaxed the words from our raw material. We also had sessions with Mary Oliver, Alan Cheuse and visiting writers.

At night we partied until the first streaks of light appeared behind the Bennington hills. Nicholas and his wife Elena invited us for dinners at their home a short walk from the campus, where we had the chance to chat with luminaries such as Jamaica Kincaid, Joyce Carol Oates, John Updike and Bernard Malamud. My husband, David, and our young daughter, Tilke, came down at weekends for readings and the parties afterwards on the lawns of Cricket Hill.

Bennington also worked its magic on my daughter. In my second year, she was eager to attend Summer Sonatina, a piano camp run by the Van Der Linde family. When I visited her she gleefully showed me the pianos in every room as well as a "secret" one concealed in a large closet.

That first term I struggled to make the crossover from non-fiction to fiction. I'd decided to write a novel based on growing up in Melbourne, Australia. Like most first novels, I did my best to disguise my own experience as I translated into fiction.

Outside the classroom, my fellow students were kind and supportive. Inside, their critiques were tough and demanding. It was difficult to let go and open up to the muse. On one occasion, Delbanco accused me of being "pathologically polite." He was right. I lay in bed at night and played and replayed my life. Finally some old, painful experiences surfaced and burst onto the page in big messy globs. A part of me which had been suppressed was springing to life.

Winter in Bennington

Then came the final term, held in the depths of winter, when most of the Bennington undergraduates were interning at publishing houses in New York or Boston. Winter in Vermont, I learned, could be as brutal as Montreal winters. We stayed in a house across from Nicholas Delbanco and all those lovely summer memories of dinner with the doors open on the gardens.

From the moment I arrived it snowed. Snow piled up either side of the country road, half covered the parked cars. The walk to the campus was a full-out battle against a howling wind and sheets of blowing snow.

The pretty white clapboard house with its dark green shutters was draughty and the fireplace in the living room alternately smoked and sucked up the heat. I came down with bronchitis. I remember being driven home to Montreal, lying on the back seat of a car, watching the icy branches against a sky the color of pewter. By the time I reached home I had pneumonia.

One morning, tossing feverishly in our bed with its spectacular view of the frozen city, I'd stared at the wallpaper with its birds and flowers. "Listen to the parrots," I mumbled to David. "We're in Madagascar." That bout of pneumonia confined me to bed for almost a month, then became an alarming winter pattern.

Later, when my doctor was adamant about my getting out to the Southwest, his words about leaving my husband for good, frightened me into action. Months of hacking through the night, followed by fever and weeks of dragging myself to work were beginning to weaken me.

My MFA novel, *The Dreams of Zoo Animals*, was published by St. Martin's Press and its reception surpassed my expectations. One morning David brought in the weekend edition of *The Washington Post* and flourished it in front of me. There on the front page, captioned *Opening Acts*, was a favorable review of my novel. We read that page together with glee. The good reviews continued. For some reason I still don't quite understand, it was translated into German. The highlight for me was my book tours. I loved connecting with my readers, who were eager to discuss their own work.

This was perhaps the acme of my writing, but it was a bittersweet celebration. *Canadian Literature*, reviewing *The Dreams of Zoo Animals*, wrote, "This novel has the intense focus and suppressed power of Virginia Woolf's early work." When my publisher sent me that review I'd been thrilled. Now however, with scarcely enough energy to sit at my desk, good reviews were of small comfort, for I knew my doctor was right. If I didn't escape the Montreal winters, that might be my last novel. But I didn't feel ready to go into exile.

Fortunately my daughter had just completed her first year at school in New Hampshire and would be there for the next two winters before she left for college. She was enjoying her new independence and encouraged me to head south. "You can't just lie around babbling on about parrots in Madagascar," I think she said.

Homesteading

After I finished my tea in the small house on Morada Lane, I lay down beside Bianca and slept until the sun slid around to the western side of the house. Then I ate the cheese and veggie sandwich I'd bought at Wild Oats in Santa Fe, hauled in the first five gallon bucket of whitewash, figured out how to gouge it open with a screwdriver, stirred the chalky mixture and took my new paintbrushes from the Randall's Lumber paper bag. By now, Bianca was sunning herself on the snow, her long elegant front paws crossed in front of her.

By the time Adam returned after a day's skiing he described as "awesome," I had banished some dreary mud-colored walls and transformed the tiny kitchen and living room. Now the light from the freshly painted white walls played against the dark beams of the low ceiling and brought out the rich warm tones of the wide-planked floor.

We headed out to devour the juicy delights of The Outback Pizza, a local watering hole where ski bums and tourists crowded in with a mixture of aging hippies.

Over the next week I completed my whitewashing. In addition to the ancient round oak table and four chairs I'd bought from the previous owner, a southwest furniture store on Pueblo del Sud yielded a small L-shaped sofa that took up most of the space in the sitting room, and two new mattresses with frames. The delivery man obligingly agreed to remove their sagging ancestors.

As his truck backed out of the parking space, the rooms felt much more cheerful. Next day I found a useful wooden island at Monet's Kitchen in the John Dunn Plaza and shortly after, at a roadside stand in Ranchos de Taos, a few doors from the flat-backed adobe church painted to fame by Georgia O'Keeffe, I discovered a pair of wooden bar stools. Now I could leave my typewriter and papers set up on the table and eat at the counter. With my favorite brass dragon lamp with the yellow glass shade I'd brought from Montreal, together with a box of books, my little house was beginning to feel like home.

Then the week was over and it was time for Adam to return to college. I drove him to the Greyhound Bus terminal for his flight back east from Albuquerque. The skiing had met his expectations, we'd explored the eateries of Taos and I'd been grateful for his company.

As the bus pulled away I had a sudden feeling of panic. Here I was in this quirky little mountain town, all alone. The only soul I knew was Maria up at Mabel's and she was busy with a new influx for a poetry workshop.

I drove back to Morada Lane, Bianca standing on the back seat peering out the window. She was my constant companion and I wouldn't have even considered my winter exile without her.

The Art of Living Alone

Married and mother of a fifteen year old daughter, I had forgotten the art of living alone. Indeed I probably had never developed this as when I married David, I had just turned twenty-one. This, I told myself, will test your resources. Think of yourself as an intrepid writer in the Southwest. Think of Mabel. I was around the same age as Mabel had been when she'd arrived in Taos. True, she'd not been alone, but had Tony Luhan and a household staff. But, as she observed in *Winter In Taos*, "If aloneness is once confronted with courage and a final giving up and relaxing into submission, acknowledging the perpetual and essential loneliness of life, whether in crowds or in deserts, there emerges a peace and contentment in one's own small domain, which emanates, really from one's own heart, coming at last home to rest."[8]

Encouraged by her words, I began to read everything I could get my hands on about the woman who'd lived up the lane at the house, which in 1991, the year of my arrival in Taos, was designated a National Historic Landmark.

I had begun my relationship with Mabel via her house, then moved on to her memoir, *Edge of Taos Desert*. Initially I was most interested in Mabel's own writing, then I discovered the excellent biography, *New Woman, New Worlds* by Lois Palken Rudnick. I devoured the details to flesh out my higgeldy-piggeldy impression of a maze of disappointing and chaotic relationships which had driven Mabel into melancholy, even attempts at suicide, and led to her psychoanalyst, A. A. Brill's, recommendation that she write.

Mabel: The Facts

Now I was ready for a coherent timeline of her life. Mabel was born, February 26, 1879, in Buffalo, New York, to Sara and Charles Ganson. Charles' father had been a dynamic part of the business boom which by the 1890s had made the town a leader in shipping and industry and produced sixty millionaires. Sara's father gave the couple, as a wedding present, a house on prestigious Delaware Avenue. Four presidents and captains of industry including the founders of Lackawanna Steel and Wells Fargo had lived on this street.

Though trained as a lawyer, Charles appears to have coasted on inherited wealth, plunging into moodiness and outbreaks of violent temper. Sara was also spoilt and moody, focusing primarily on controlling those about her and running a tight ship.

Mabel grew up in an atmosphere of parental arguing and coldness, big on outward appearances. Raised essentially by her nursemaid, she recalls, "Probably most people have some memories of their earliest years that contain a little warmth and liveliness, but in my own I cannot find one happy hour. I have no recollection of my mother's ever giving me a kiss or smile of spontaneous affection, or any sign from my father except dark looks and angry sound."[9]

On one occasion, when her mother took the little girl to New York, they stayed in a hotel. Mabel recalls her fear of being abandoned when her mother went out for the evening with her friend, Randolph, leaving her daughter alone, to try to sleep between cold linen sheets.

Though her home life was cold and cheerless, she enjoyed the company of her young friends, including her neighbor, little Nina Rumsey Wilcox. It's clear that Mabel, even at a young age liked to take charge. She wrote, "I liked playing with Nina. I could make her do as I liked. She was always obedient." When her grandfather presented her with a pony, Cupid, and a two-seated cart, she and her friends took off to explore the delights of nearby Forest Lawn Cemetery, the enormous park designed by Frederick Olmstead.

At St. Margaret's School she took drawing lessons every Thursday with Miss Rose Clark. "I enjoyed her special kind of vision," wrote Mabel. "I liked to enter her world and see life through her eyes. She saw nothing but beauty, all the rest she ignored." Rose Clark clearly helped lay down the groundwork for Mabel's lifelong pursuit of artistic beauty and years later, the two women remained friends.

Summing up her Buffalo childhood, Mabel wrote, "Even with all its melancholy, my childhood had a wild, sweet enthralling zestfulness."

Mabel's "coming out" ball was attended by one thousand guests. She refused to dance. When after the ball, she and her mother drove the short distance to their house, her mother remarked, "Well, that's over with."[10]

One of the first things people seemed to know about Mabel was her four marriages, so it was not surprising to learn that Mabel's main interest in men was "discovering my effect upon them, instead of responding to their feeling for me."[11] From the start, she noticed that she appeared to have a "strange power" over them, a power which she refers to many times in her writings, a sort of "inner force" that both attracted them to her, then in the way of a muse, inspired them. Mabel developed a curious ability to put into words, men's ideas more eloquently than they themselves could verbalize.

At twenty-one, she married Karl Evans, with whom she rode. He worked at the Anchor Line Steamship Company, where his father was president. The marriage started out as a game to get Karl away from the girl to whom he was engaged. Mabel succeeded, but as it turned out, she was the victim of events. Karl, suitably infatuated by Mabel's power moves, played a trick to trap her. He lured her on an outing, then escorted her into a church where he'd arranged for the minister to marry them. Mabel describes how she "began to tremble and look desperately behind" her, but Karl's best hunting friend was standing right there. "I could no more have managed to escape past that determined, dangerous man than…a rabbit."[12]

However, when Mabel's father violently opposed the marriage, Mabel, to spite him, agreed with her mother's plans for a formal church wedding. The young couple moved into a small white house near her parents. She describes her marriage to Karl as "A limited, friendly marriage so inarticulate in expression…with so little to say to him about my inner life and thoughts and feelings."[13]

After one miscarriage, Mabel gave birth to a baby boy, John, who weighed an outsized thirteen pounds. Though she enjoyed her pregnancy, when she woke from the pain and chloroform of birth, her response to her son was not as she had anticipated.

"I didn't feel anything for it. I saw it was a nice baby but it didn't seem to be mine. I felt sorry for myself and wounded all over my life. It seemed to me I didn't want a baby after all."

The birth was followed by three traumatic events. A few weeks after the birth, Mabel, visiting her parents' house, heard her father call from his bedroom. "I'm awfully sick," he moaned as his breath came faster. I wish I had a cross. Do you think you could find me a cross in this house?" Cold as ice, without a single throb of response in me anywhere, I said, "I'll look." I didn't feel anything."[14]

Her father died painfully in the early hours of that next morning. Later that same year, Mabel was in bed for ten days recovering from an operation to correct a prolapsed uterus when she was summoned to her husband's side in hospital. He'd been accidentally shot by his friend while hunting. Both Mabel and her mother were now widows, Mabel, mother of a baby less than a year old.

To escape depression and the scandal induced by a brief sexual relationship with her married gynecologist, her mother packed her off to Paris with the baby and two nurses, one to care for little John, the other to look after her.

On the crossing, she met wealthy Boston architect, Edwin Dodge. A kind and cheerful man, he offered her security and luxury, and baby John, a loving father. Mostly, she speculates, for security, she agreed to marry Dodge, though she told him she wasn't in love with him and felt no desire except to have him around to help her make something new and beautiful.

They did. They married and bought the sun-filled fifteenth century Medici built, Villa Curonia near Florence. Dodge designed the remodeling, Mabel threw herself, body and soul into creating an exquisite interior where nothing was selected or positioned without thought and tremendous care to detail, creating a life dedicated to art and beauty. Rose Clark, the art teacher who had inspired the pursuit of beauty those Thursdays at St. Margaret's School in Buffalo, became one of Mabel's advisors as she created her masterpiece. "It's almost like a love affair, the drama over an antique."[15]

From the midnight blue bedroom to her pale grey and yellow sitting room, to the "Gran" salon, where the firelight played on silks and velvets, polished silver, fine antiques and vases of fresh flowers, each room fully absorbed Mabel's attention.

Once done, she threw herself into "collecting" interesting people. She welcomed to her salons, Gertrude and her brother, Leo, Alice B. Toklas, Andre Gide, Bernard Berenson and an assortment of European royalty. Later, as her marriage to Edwin became drab and unfulfilling, she writes, "What a universe between him and me! I so deep, so fatal, and so glamorous—and he so ordinary and matter-of-fact! Little does he guess of the layers upon layers of perceptions of understanding, of feeling for things that I carry locked in me!"[16]

In spite of the energy she poured into the Villa Curonia, the finished house failed to make her feel truly at home. Though she had been successful in creating an enchanting interior, she felt, "a fatigue from straining myself to fill an empty form that could be blown into a fullness for a while, but that would always collapse when one ceased to blow it up."[17]

After eight years in Europe, Mabel observed that the people she knew in Florence were to her no more than "portraits in a picture gallery."

It was, she decided, time to return to New York and send John to an appropriate school. As she stood with her son on the deck as the ship approached New York, she took his hand and began to sob, "Remember, it is ugly in America. Remember we have left everything worthwhile behind us. America is all machinery and moneymaking and factories—it is ugly, ugly, ugly! Never forget that!"

When she had finished, her son said in a small, firm voice, "I don't think it's so ugly."[18]

After setting up an apartment at 23 Fifth Avenue, Mabel decorated every room white on white. Edwin went each day to his office to "practice" his architecture. The apartment was at the fashionable end of Greenwich Village, just a few blocks from Alfred Stieglitz's "291," the center of the avant-garde movement in America. Later, she would invite Stieglitz's wife, Georgia O'Keeffe and her friend Rebecca Strand, wife of photographer Paul, to stay with her in Taos.

The year 1913 was an exciting time in New York. It seemed to Mabel, that "barriers went down and people reached each other who had never been in touch before; there were all sorts of new ways to communicate, as well as new communications. The new spirit was abroad and swept us all together."[19] She considered herself, essentially an instrument of the times, with her talent for bringing people together.

Mabel's Wednesday salons attracted a swell of movers and shakers of the day including writers, artists, poets, lawyers, psychoanalysts, politicians and intellectuals from all walks of life. Radical feminist Emma Goldman and birth-control advocate Margaret Sanger jump-started passionate discussions around the nuts and bolts of women's issues; emancipation from the confining roles of the day both social and political, equal educational opportunities, day-care, birth control, venereal disease, sexual expression and fulfillment.

In the resulting publicity which followed her article in *Arts and Decoration*, Mabel helped fund and put together in New York, the exhibition of emerging European modernist painters, The Armory Show. While the artists were male, 80% of the donors were women. Mabel wrote of the avant-garde show which would be so controversial, "It became, overnight, my own little Revolution. I would upset America;

I would, with fatal irrevocable disaster to the old order of things. I was going to dynamite New York and nothing would stop me. Well, nothing did."[20]

Mabel was effectively launched as the epitome of the "New Woman."

Following a series of separations, her marriage to Edwin Dodge wound down, followed by a flurry of new relationships.

She, like other women rebelling against the old order, pursued a pattern of what was now expected of the "new woman", the freedom to seek the sexual expression men for generations have taken for granted. Her turbulent relationships led to an intense interlude with Harvard educated, self-styled communist, John Reed, who would later write about the Russian Revolution, in *Ten Days That Shook The World*.

Mabel discovered that with her powerful inner force, she could inspire Reed in his quest to liberate the working man. She delayed sex with him "to preserve the intense life we had created together without (as I felt it would be) descending into the mortality of love. Something in me adored the high clear excitement of continence, and the tension that came from our carnalized vitality."[21]

When finally they became lovers, Mabel experienced what activist Margaret Sanger described as "the first duty of men and women, with the body so illumined and conscious that it would be able to express in all its parts the language of the spirit's pleasure."[22] However, Mabel's sexual delight gave way to vulnerability and jealousy, as Reed continued to fill his days afield gathering material for his articles in *The Masses*. Nor was he faithful. "Reed and I love each other so, that's why we torment each other," she wrote, conjuring images of a *Wuthering Heights,* Catherine-Heathcliffe savagery.

She sensed that infidelity was the death knell to love, and pondered how her discomfort with this fit with developing feminism. "Are we supposed to 'make' men do things? Are men to change? Is monogamy better than polygamy?"[23]

Inevitably, the infancy of feminism was filled with contradictions. On one hand, women no longer wanted to be viewed only in terms of reproduction, but like many of the women who went west to escape "nervous breakdowns," Mabel carried with her the sense that sexual liberation should incorporate becoming a muse who would inspire men to fully bring forth their creative genius.

Mabel, who early on expressed strong feelings against being "idle," wrote that she felt "functional and helpful and constructive to life" only when her inner force was being used to aid Reed in his work. Reed had told her in the early days of the time they spent together in Florence, that her life force was so strong it was "like being near some highly charged electrical battery, from which one could draw electricity and become enormously strengthened."[24] It would be many decades before the idea of women fueling their own creativity with such inner force would be acceptable.

Eventually, Mabel could not cope with the emotional turbulence of the relationship and twice attempted suicide in Florence. When she and Reed returned to America, he found that traveling with a wealthy socialite with "fourteen different kinds of pills," made him uneasy, as he championed the workers of the day. The relationship began its downward curve.

Mabel turned her attention to other men, including critic and writer Carl Van Vechten and painter Andrew Dasburg, who attended her salons and produced the portrait, "Presence of Mabel Dodge."

John Reed, however, was not entirely out of the picture. After a trip to Colorado to cover a coal miners' strike, Reed, his affection for Mabel strengthened by separation, surfaced with renewed ardor and spent the summer with her and the Greenwich Village set in Provincetown.

Mabel met the Russian free-form dancer, Isadora Duncan, and watched her perform with the little children she had brought with her from Russia. She also met Isadora's sister, Elizabeth, and the children of her school, a learning environment dedicated to all forms of beauty, including the music of Schubert and Schumann, poetry, movement, a careful diet and self-discipline.

Mabel found and donated to, the perfect home for the school, set at Croton-on-Hudson. Around this time, she appeared to re-examine her feelings of motherhood. When her son was born, she had had no feeling left over to give him and all "through his first years of babyhood, it was as though I had been away from him, though he was always right there. I never knew John as a baby."[25] Around this time, on a visit to an orphanage, she took under her wing a girl of around eight, "little Elizabeth," whom she enrolled in the school and, though she did not adopt the child, she continued to support her.

Shortly after helping Elizabeth Duncan locate her school, Mabel rented a nearby farmhouse in Croton, called Finney Farm. A. A. Brill's opinions notwithstanding, she appears to have found peace and pleasure in country life foreshadowing her attraction to life in Taos.

In May 1915, she met Russian émigré artist, Maurice Sterne who, more than any artist she had ever known, "craved assurance." She saw in him a potential for sculpture and threw her support behind this, encouraging him, buying him clay, offering him a studio in an empty lifeguard station, when he accompanied her to Provincetown. When he made the inevitable advance, she said, "No, Maurice, it's your work I'm interested in, not you!", thereby increasing his attraction to her.

In 1917, Sterne became her third husband. Marie Howe, the suffragette told Mabel. "I suppose I should congratulate you. Probably everyone else will. But I can't help feeling a little sad. You have counted so much for women. Your example has stood for courage and strength! You had the nerve to live your own life openly and frankly—to take a lover if you wished without hiding under the law. You have shown women they had the right to live as they chose. But Now! When I think of the disappointment in the whole women's world today!"[26] she exclaimed.

Shortly after the marriage, Mabel collapsed into the melancholy she'd experienced following both her previous marriages to Karl Evans and to Edwin Dodge, triggered by feelings of being trapped. She encouraged Sterne to go west and search for new subject matter. From Santa Fe, he urged her to join him for the good of her health. She did. Interestingly, her son, John, who went to Santa Fe with Sterne, some time earlier had developed, with his friend, Boyce Hapgood, a real passion for all things Western. The two boys "cultivated hard, ruthless expressions and thrust out their lower jaws." Young John was delighted to go west.

She was not attracted to Santa Fe and chose to journey north to Taos, where she was soon joined by Sterne and John. Not long after her arrival in Taos, on a visit to the Pueblo, she was invited into one of the houses by a beautiful woman, Candelaria, whose husband, Tony was singing softly in an inner room. The events unfolded with a mystical quality. Some time earlier, Mabel had dreamed of a man but the face had been unfamiliar. The moment she saw Tony, she realized that it had been his face in her dream. An extraordinary bond formed between Mabel and Tony, and eventually Maurice returned to New York, from where, in 1922, he divorced Mabel. Five years after their meeting at the Pueblo, Tony divorced Candelaria. He and Mabel married in 1923. The same year, Mabel's son, John Evans, now in his early twenties, married "little Alice," daughter of Santa Fe poet, Alice Corbin Henderson and artist, architect, William Penhallow Henderson, maker of the handsome black and sienna colored tiles in the dining room at the Big House.

Though the marriage inevitably was far from smooth sailing, this time the union appeared to give Mabel, for the first time, the emotional stability which she craved. Unlike her previous relationships, Tony did not wish to tap into her mysterious inner force. He appeared to live a rich inner life of his own for which he made many night trips for ceremony at the Pueblo and into the mountains. Mabel was free to enjoy life at her own pace, to invite her friends to visit, to savor the beauty of nature and become a serious writer.

The couple were at their best as they shared their love of the land and the daily details of living in harmony with nature. Mabel delighted in the bounty brought by each season as the pantry filled with the fruit and vegetables grown on the property and on Tony's ranch outside the village. They remained married until Mabel's death in 1962.

I kept returning to *Edge of Taos Desert* and to Mabel's responses to a strange new life with her well-tuned eye and ear. I enjoyed her incisive candor and was delighted to read about her first viewing of the land on which men from the Pueblo built her house from bricks of mud, the land on which my studio stood.

Not long after her arrival in Taos, where she stayed at the house of the eccentric Englishman, Arthur Manby with Sterne and cowboy-aspiring John, Tony showed Mabel a piece of land he thought she should buy. "This is the nicest place I know 'cept the Pueblo. Little bit high up, good air, and you see all over." He waved his hand across the south and west and north where we could see the whole valley stretching out beyond the town, and the sacred mountain looming dark and secret, so solid there at one side where it faced the narrow southern canyon entrance up from the outer world, over across the level sage-brush land, eighteen miles away."[27]

A Bridge Between Two Cultures

Mabel bought twelve acres of that land including the original four room adobe "shaped like a coffin," which slowly grew into the existing twenty-two room Big House, five guest houses and gatehouse. The house was a joint project. Tony designed and supervised the exterior, Mabel the interior details. She continued to send Maurice Sterne a monthly check for the four years until she married Lujan. She changed the spelling to Luhan for more convenient pronunciation.

The new couple lived together in the property which Mabel named Los Gallos, after the brightly colored ceramic roosters mounted along the roofline. Unofficially it became known as the Big House. In 1948 they moved across Morada Lane to a smaller house in which they remained until her death. Tony returned to the Pueblo where he died in January 1963, just five months after Mabel's death.

Mabel described her pre-Taos life and nature as "spoiled and distorted" and seized the chance to establish what she envisioned as a "new world plan", based not on the "raging lust for individuality..like everyone else on earth" but for a deeper connection with others and with the land. This longing for connection attracted her so deeply to the Pueblo.

She hoped, through her marriage to Antonio Lujan, to build a "bridge between two cultures." Ansel Adams, who spent time at the Big House, once rather cattily observed that Mabel had "talons for talent" and over the next forty years she would invite and nurture writers, painters, and photographers; Dorothy Brett, Maynard Dixon, Willa Cather, Dorothea Lange, D. H. Lawrence, Georgia O'Keeffe, Paul and Rebecca Strand, Frank Waters, Edward Weston and choreographer Martha Graham.

Most of the artistic rebels and innovators of the time appear to have visited 240 Morada Lane. Disillusioned by the carnage of WWI, they were eager to embrace a new way of being. Refreshed by the clear light and high mountain air, they were free to explore this new world as they chose. Some would stay longer than planned, others returned frequently. A few, like O'Keeffe, Frieda Lawrence, Dorothy Brett and Frank Waters, made their permanent home in New Mexico.

The spirit of place influenced each of them to translate the light and the scenes at the Pueblo into image, word and movement, fulfilling, at least visually, Mabel's desire for that bridge between two cultures. Maynard Dixon alone, made forty paintings when Mabel gave him and his wife, Dorothea Lange, one of her houses from 1931–1932. O'Keeffe, charmed by her four months at Mabel's in the summer of 1929, made her permanent home in the village of Abiquiu.

Though the history of 240 Morada Lane was glamorous and intriguing, I was more interested in Mabel's own writings about her life at the Big House. In the following winters, I continued to reread *Edge of Taos Desert* and *Winter in Taos*. I was living alone, Mabel with her husband, Tony, and a household staff, but the connection with her writing made me feel some sort of sisterhood with this woman who had left the east coast and created a rich and meaningful life in New Mexico. In short, I chose Mabel as my inspiration.

A few days after my young friend, Adam's, departure, I strolled down Morada Lane, past the adobe wall next door painted with faded angels, past glimpses of small houses behind *latilla* fences, each with its large wood pile, past the little path of trampled earth that led into Kit Carson Park and past the tumbledown shack at the place where mud met paving. The snow of early morning was already melting beneath the bright sunshine. By afternoon it would be mud.

At The Taos Book Shop

The Taos Book Shop, in its own little courtyard off Kit Carson, proclaimed itself the oldest bookstore west of the Mississippi. As I stepped down, careful not to bump my head on the low beam, the warmth from a generous fireplace embraced me. A large grey cat dozed on the hearth and every possible surface breathed books old and new.

The woman in the Scandinavian sweater, behind the counter, had curly blonde hair and friendly blue eyes.

"Take your time," she welcomed. She must have sensed my need for a haven, for she added, "Stay as long as you want."

As I browsed the books on Mabel Dodge Luhan, we chatted. I told her about my house on Morada Lane. "I know your house," She said. Her name was Susanna. "It's charming. I looked at it before I decided on a new house out on Blueberry Hill. It's lovely out there with that view of the mountain."

As the day wore on I ate a veggie sandwich a few doors up Kit Carson at Caffé Tazza, where locals sprawled with notebooks and newspapers on well worn couches in the sunny back room. The ubiquitous red geraniums, which Mabel observed were brought to Mexico by the Spanish, then by the Mexicans to Taos, thrived in large terracotta pots along the windows.

After lunch I returned to the bookstore. It was a slow day and Susanna and I resumed our conversation.

She'd relocated from Pennsylvania the previous year. "My mother came out here in the twenties," she told me. "She was a painter from an artistic family and she was having a relationship with Kenneth Adams, one of the Taos Society of Artists."

At the end of the day I asked Susanna, "Will you be my friend?"

"I'd love to be your friend, Valmai," she said. As it turned out, Susanna Tvede and I would become staunch friends and visit Taos together twenty-five years later.

That evening, after Susanna closed the bookstore, we walked downtown and celebrated at Tapas of Taos, a hole-in-the-wall at the foot of Bent Street, with hot pink and turquoise walls, decorated Day-of-the-Dead style with rakish skeletons. I was curious about Susanna's mother, who had been in Taos during Mabel's early years on Morada Lane.

"Tell me about her," I said as we savored our plate of black olives and green chili goat cheese.

Susanna's Mother: The Taos Society Of Artists

"My mother's maiden name was Claudine Kraenzlein," Susanna told me. " She had attended The George School, a Quaker boarding school in Newtown, Pennsylvania. Her roommate and best friend, Bobbi Hawk's family owned the Hawk Ranch in Taos. That was the land that Mabel Dodge Luhan bought part of and gave to D. H. Lawrence. I think his wife, Frieda, gave Mabel the manuscript for *Sons and Lovers* in exchange.

"He called it the Kiowa Ranch. Now it's owned by the University of New Mexico and it's known as the Lawrence Ranch.

"After she finished at the George School, Mother went on to the Art Students' League in New York. That was where she met Kenneth Adams.

"In the summer of nineteen twenty-four, Bobbi Hawk invited Mother to stay with her at the family ranch in Taos. By that time, Kenneth Adams had also gone west. He'd connected with Andrew Dasburg the artist, and Dasburg became his mentor. Dasburg was a friend of Mabel's, he'd done a portrait of her back in New York. Adams and Dasburg used to go way out onto the land for weeks on end to paint the wilds of New Mexico.

"Adams and my mother met again in Taos and when she returned to New York they exchanged a series of love letters," Susanna told me. "My mother was so young, just twenty one and he was six years older.

His family had been supporting him but that was about to come to an end. He told my mother that he couldn't afford a serious relationship, even though they genuinely seemed to care for each other. At that point, it turned out painting was his singular passion. In nineteen twenty-six The Taos Society of Artists invited him to become their eighth and youngest member. Later he taught at the University of New Mexico."

Susanna, also a talented painter, with one of her works in the permanent collection at Bryn Mawr College, had visited Taos several times, drawn there in her mother's footsteps.

"I loved going to end of the world places," she told me with a laugh. "I remember a trip where I drove to Taos with some friends and going along a section of the old wooden sidewalk near the Plaza. Later we walked out on the road towards the Pueblo. It felt so good and we sat down on a wall and there were grasshoppers all around us in this dusty old place.

"Later I went out by myself on a Greyhound bus. When my mother was in Taos she'd been friends with Dorothy Brett, the English painter. Actually she was the Honorable Dorothy, she'd been part of the Bloomsbury circle and she'd come out to Taos with D. H. and Frieda Lawrence. Brett and Mabel Dodge Luhan were friends and I think Mabel supported her at the end.

"Frieda invited my mother and Bobbi up to the ranch for tea. D. H. was there when they arrived but then later he went off by himself on his donkey. Brett was living in that little shack right at the back of the house and she came in for tea. I can picture them together and I think they had a lot of fun.

"It was that afternoon Brett gave my mother one of her paintings and I'd brought a photo of it with me when I first came to Taos. I took it down to the Harwood Museum on LeDoux Street and showed it to the curator, David Witt. He was very interested in my mother's correspondence with Kenneth Adams."

Later, she showed me a photograph of Brett's gift to her mother. It was a small painting of the back of a Pueblo woman, standing; wide white pants beneath a long pale pink skirt, a filmy black headscarf cascading down her back. She holds a woven basket high above her head and a ray of golden light bathes her. In the background you can see two of those tiny square Pueblo windows and a section of the cone shaped fireplace. Why is she facing away from the viewer? What is she looking at? I liked the painting for its mystical allure and was curious about the woman who'd painted it.

"After I moved into the house on Blueberry Hill, " Susanna told me, "one day I walked into The Taos Book Shop. The owner, Deborah, and her mother, Barbara, were there. Barbara was wearing all this gorgeous silver and turquoise jewelry, and we talked about my mother's time in Taos. Barbara was interested that Mother's roommate at the George School had been Bobbi Hawk, as Barbara's grandmother had had a Hawk connection.

"We had a long and interesting conversation about those connections. Later they offered me a job at the bookshop," Susanna finished.

My morning walk with Bianca up to Mabel's to visit "my mountain," was a fine way to start the day. As we headed up the lane we'd hear the customary ringing of an axe chopping wood and the barking of dogs. Out there amid the sage, rose a large white wooden cross which, I was to learn, O'Keeffe painted as "Black Cross."

Later I read that the cross had been erected by the Penitentes, a cult whose original meeting house, or "*morada*" had been moved from the lane on which I lived, to the edge of pueblo land several lanes over. The Penitentes had practiced self-flagellation and had performed simulated crucifixions. Some hinted darkly that not all had been simulated, but I was not drawn to learn more.

Mabel wrote, "Sometimes in the night, the singing voices wake me when they are marching up to the Calvary. There is a thud-thud that punctuates the wild anguish of the chant. The land has been turned into a different place, the underworld rises and invades the darkness, and a spirit is abroad that has its habitation in the depths."[28]

Though I never heard, nor did I wish to hear, the "wild anguish" of nocturnal chanting, sometimes Bianca would growl and pace at the window. Several times the motion detector light I had installed just outside the gate to the parking area, would come on and I would watch from the darkness. Perhaps it was some small creature, maybe just the wind in the lilac tree by the gate. After a while Bianca would jump up beside me and we would drift off to sleep. "Women have to be careful in this town," a woman at Caffé Tazza warned me. "We don't walk alone at night." I was careful to heed her dark words.

Fortunately I had Bianca. I trusted my big silver borzoi to take care of me, but I was careful to keep the gate locked and on the rare occasions when I ventured out after dark, she always accompanied me. Sometimes the two of us walked out to the edge of the desert just before sunset to watch the snowy crags turn pink then deep red. Apparently the mountains received their name when Spanish explorer, Coronado, entered the valley at sunset. When he saw the light on the snow he exclaimed "*Sangre de Christo!*" Blood of Christ!

At the Pueblo

A rutted path, frozen in the morning, then turning to mud later in the day, led to the cross and I'd peer over the fence, wishing I could let Bianca run free.

"Why don't you ask them at the Pueblo?" suggested Maria. So one crispy morning I drove north a short distance from town, took the right fork at *Allsup's Convenience and Gas* and drove about a mile past small adobe houses and fields of wiry, rough-coated horses.

I stood just inside the adobe wall of the Pueblo beside the little whitewashed church of St. Geronimo, and stared. Ahead of me two piles of building stood against the base of the majestic snow-covered mountain, a series of brown adobe cubes rising pyramid-style to the fifth floor, with tiny square windows, the only access floor-to-floor, rough hand-hewn wooden ladders.

The entire structure made from earth and straw, wood and water, felt so much a part of the land and sheltering mountain. A few women in long skirts and shawls were fetching water from the stream which divided the two buildings into north and south.

This Pueblo of the Tiwa speaking people has been continuously inhabited for a thousand years. Though most of almost two thousand people of the Pueblo live in the low adobe houses I had passed on my way in, currently about one hundred and fifty still lived in its small dark cubes. With no electricity or running water, they heated by piñon fires and used the water which gushes down into the stream from the sacred Blue Lake high on the mountain, twenty two miles above the village.

In 1906, the United States had taken away 48,000 acres of their land for the National Forest. Under president Richard Nixon, in 1970, the land was returned to the Pueblo and in 1992 it became a World Heritage Site, joining the likes of the Taj Mahal, the Great Pyramids and the Grand Canyon. Today the 99,000 acres of the Pueblo, including the Blue Lake of the Sacred Mountain, part of the Sangre de Christo range, are off-limits to all but the people of the Pueblo, protecting their natural resources and ceremonies.

Doing Nothing

Mabel had been deeply affected by her visits to the Pueblo. "It was as though the Pueblo had an invisible wall around it, separating the Indians from the world we knew—a wall that kept their life safe within it, like a fire that cannot spread. How self-contained it seems! I thought, and how contented it feels! I mused to myself. I wish I belonged in there."[29]

Over the next twelve years I would also be drawn regularly to the Pueblo. I liked it best just before it closed in late winter and early spring for ceremonial retreat. At that time there was a certain dreamy quality with very few visitors. The best time was in the morning when it felt so quiet and serene. I think I was attracted not just by its apparent deep fusion with the mountain and the sage plains, but because it comforted me. Somehow, as the world raced ahead filled with new technology and an ever-increasing effort to cram as much as possible into your day, when people said, "I'm so busy," with evident pride, the Pueblo and its way of life, though change inevitably lapped outside the walls, felt solid, deeply rooted.

In my new world far from days punctuated by phone calls and meetings, the possibility of "being," rather than "doing," now attracted me. I recalled how much I had enjoyed as a child, what A. A. Milne's, Christopher Robin described as "doing nothing." Consequently, I was delighted when I read Mabel's realization that her pleasure was "in being very still and sensing things."

She did however recognize the importance of contrasts. "Still and all, if one hadn't done a lot of things and been through all the movements of life, one wouldn't have this fund of experience to draw on, or be able to sense all the many experienced pleasures and delights and pains and worries, too, that are suggested by the sights from my window, by the things about me in the room, by the odors and memories and associations that are the essences of activity and that, like poetry, are now the emotions of activity remembered in tranquility."[30]

During Pueblo visiting hours, some of the ground floor rooms, their wooden doors painted sky blue or turquoise, opened to sell handmade items; silver jewelry, pottery flecked with the mica found in the earth nearby, drums and woven rugs. You could also munch delicious fry-bread and listen to native flutes as you wandered around. Several years after my arrival, for my birthday, I splurged on a silver conch belt, made to measure by Sonny Spruce.

Mabel wrote, "How faint the life of Italian earth seemed to me as I recalled it; how faint and dim and dying out. And New York! Why, when I remembered that clamor and movement, the rumble of New York came back to me and the impotent and despairing protest of a race that has long gone wrong and is caught in a trap. How unhappy, how horribly unhappy, the memory of the sound of New York was in my ears!"[31]

My feelings about Montreal were less intense. Though my memories of winter, holed up in a vast and draughty bedroom above the frozen city, tended to the morbid, I had only pleasant memories of sidewalk cafés in summer. The clamor of the city stimulated me. I'd had a little writing studio on *Carre St.Louis* and I loved exploring the architecture of an old city and the narrow streets around my studio.

Yet after a lifetime filled to the brim with, as David put it," romance, travel and adventure," this unexpected solitude in an unfamiliar place was a gift. A time that had begun as no more than an escape from illness, was unfolding with an unfamiliar feeling I decided was contentment.

Unlike Mabel, I was never able to view the sacred Blue Lake, but years after my arrival in Taos, on a gloriously clear winter day, I was thrilled to receive an unexpected gift. My plane was flying from Albuquerque to Chicago. I looked out the window hoping to catch a glimpse of Taos. Suddenly the sunlight glinted on a little lake the color of sapphires, set in a snow-covered mountain.

"You're welcome to walk your dog out there," the governor of the Pueblo told me. "But be careful. There are some characters you wouldn't want to meet."

He didn't go into further detail. I figured early morning would be pretty safe. Desperados, if they planned their wanderings, generally prowl in the cover of night.

Next morning I finally stepped over the section of barbed wire fencing that separated Mabel's from the wilderness of the pueblo. Bianca surged ahead and disappeared into the sage. I wasn't worried. She never strayed far. When she reappeared she ran, stretched into a long white line, past the cross, where she paused and looked back at me. The smell of the sage heavy with dew was invigorating, the snow beneath each bush melted from the natural oils.

Overhead the sky turned that improbable blue and the sun began to melt the snow. I stood out there and for the first time since my arrival felt a sense of childlike happiness. This had not been a mistake.

Later, as I savored Mabel's memoirs of her first year in Taos, I was delighted to learn of her similar response to this high bright place.

"I found out that the sunshine in New Mexico could do almost anything with one," she wrote. "Make one well if one felt ill or change a dark mood and lighten it. It entered into one's deepest places and melted the thick, slow densities. It made one feel good. That is, alive."[32]

In Montreal, once the temperature sank below freezing in late November, early December if you were lucky, that was it for the day. In Taos, winter temperatures can climb from twenty degrees to the fifties in one morning and by noon, you're ready to strip your layers and enjoy the sun in a tee shirt.

As I watched Bianca romp and sniff on the pueblo land, I marveled that in spite of the snow and cold, I hadn't had so much as a sore throat or sniffle and my dark afternoons broken only by the lamp for Seasonal Affective Disorder, were receding into that other life.

One morning at Caffé Tazza one of the regulars asked me, "What brought you to Taos?" "Bronchitis," I answered. "I've had it every winter since I was a little kid. My doctor told me I needed to come to the Southwest."

"Your doctor was smart. Around here they say that Taos is a healing place for lung diseases. Actually it's a good place if you have any illness, that's why there are so many healers in town." She scribbled some names in her notebook, tore out the page and gave it to me. "You should start with Mary Tara up on Dragoon Lane. She's awesome."

As I continued my reading, including the fascinating book, *Ladies of the Canyons,* by Lesley Poling-Kempes, I discovered that in the first decades of the twentieth century there began a flow of women and men with respiratory ailments, including tuberculosis, drawn to the salubrious climate of New Mexico. Santa Fe's Saint Vincent's Hospital opened the Sunmount Sanatorium with views of the small park beside the Cathedral of St. Francis and down the street, the plaza.

Less fortunate were those who moved to New Mexico and, convinced that the sunshine and high dry air were all they needed to overthrow the bacillus, plunged into a vigorous life on the range. In primitive surroundings and without the necessary rest, many did not survive.

Along with those with respiratory ailments, the exodus of east coast rebels swelled until the second World War. Unable to find a balance between the old restraints and their quest for a new freedom, they, like Mabel and young Miriam Hapgood, victims of "nervous breakdown," discovered a new, more tolerant life in the Southwest.

At the Pinch Penny Wash 'O' Mat: The Other Taos

I was beginning to feel at home in my new winter town. When the laundry hamper overflowed, the Pinch Penny Wash 'O' Mat came to my rescue and I enjoyed chatting with other women as we watched our clothes swirl in the suds. Many of the women turned out to be writers and artists from elsewhere who worked irregular hours at the galleries and cafés. It was here that I first encountered evidence of a darker side to Taos.

"You know, people come to Taos expecting it to be all O'Keeffe and D. H. Lawrence and parties and making wonderful art" one woman told me as we listened to the rhythmic chugging of our washing machines. "For most of us it's not like that at all. We're drawn here by all the stories, but what you don't hear is Taos is a poor town. The reality is if you're trying to make a living as well as art, it can be tough. You take what you can get and often you're so damned tired from waiting tables in town and up at the Ski Valley, trying to pay the rent, you just don't have any energy left over to write or paint or whatever." Then for some reason she added, "I nearly got hit by a drunk driver coming down from the Ski Valley one night. I could have been killed."

For a moment I felt guilty that to date my Taos experience had revolved around the privileged history of Mabel's. Still, I comforted myself, you've worked hard all your life and now you're living on your savings for the first time. It's not as though you're some sort of dilettante.

I turned to her. "I came here because if I'd stayed back east I might have died of lung problems. That can affect your heart, you know."

I was pleased when she looked at me with more kindred spirit.

"Oh, you're one of them," she said.

"Do you think you'll stay?" I asked. She looked surprised. "Of course, " she sounded indignant. "Where else am I going to find views like this? You just have to stay here long enough to do the work on yourself, you know what I mean?"

"I just got here," I told her.

She grinned. "Don't worry, you'll find out. The Mountain makes itself pretty clear. It either accepts you or spits you out."

I became a regular at Cid's health food market, where the smell of fresh rotisserie chicken mingled with local sage and cedar, tied in bundles with colorful thread. Later, a new café, *The Wild and Natural*, provided a welcome relief from my own uninspired dinners which revolved around soup, sardines and avocados. When I read that Mabel always had loaves of freshly baked bread on her table, my fondness for her was complete. I enjoyed reading about the picnics Mabel and Tony took with their friends, riding out into the pristine land, stopping for lunch by a stream. Tony was an excellent camp cook.

I lingered on the descriptions of her various entertaining.

"Bourbon and grapefruit juice and mint leaves freshly picked along the ditch, shaken up with ice cubes until the glass shaker is frosty, and along with this, summer muslins and perfume, laughter and fun, with the antagonisms forgotten for a moment and everyone gathered together in good humor.

"As likely as not we will have lamb for dinner, brought down from Tony's ranch at Tienditas, potatoes grown at the same place, baked squash with raisins in the hollow, lettuce and cucumbers and tomato salad with imported oil and lemon dressing, and for dessert, a brown Betty pudding with hard sauce.

"When we have squabs from the dovecotes out in the garden, and small creamed onions, shoestring potatoes and crabapple jelly, and in addition, just for fun, broiled mushrooms, with a salad of celery and nuts and apples smeared with home-made mayonnaise dressing, one can feel one's cup is just about running over, especially with a cheesecake for dessert."[33]

Indeed! I missed family dinners, sharing the day and chatting over my husband's delicious meals. In fact I struggled with the evenings. I was used to working in the day, but by evening on Morada Lane, when it grew dark early in winter, I walked a fine line between solitude and loneliness.

I decided to take Bianca out past Mabel's at sunset, eat around six, then enjoy an hour on the phone with David who was two hours later. Before I climbed into bed to read, Bianca and I would stand in the garden and admire the night sky. In Montreal, moon and stars were obliterated by city lights. Here however, in the thin clear mountain air, I never tired of marveling at the sea of glittering stars and the phases of the moon.

By the time I finished reading, it was eight o'clock. Often I'd fall asleep to the music from the skating rink in Kit Carson Park on the other side of my back fence. The upside of this early bedtime was the early morning when I'd wake before dawn and watch the light flush behind the mountains. As I compared notes with Susanna, I discovered she followed similar patterns in the evening, indeed on the few occasions when we went to a movie or any event at the Taos Community Center, which went past eight, we'd joke about our "nightlife."

The Forbidden Paintings

High on our list of "nightlife" were outings to the old-fashioned downstairs cinema on the plaza, across from the five and dime and a few doors from The Hotel La Fonda. One afternoon after a matinee, I wandered into the cavernous lobby of La Fonda. I had read about the collection of what had come to be known as *The Forbidden Paintings*, by D. H. Lawrence and now locked in a small room off the lobby. Who wouldn't be curious?

In 1929, the year after D.H. Lawrence's *Lady Chatterley's Lover* was received with shock and loathing, London police seized nine paintings from The Dorothy Warren Gallery. *The Observer* described the paintings as "frankly disgusting," *The Daily Telegraph*, as "gross and obscene."

Lawrence wrote that he painted "no picture that won't shock peoples' castrated social spirituality...the phallus is a great sacred image: it represents a deep, deep life which has been denied in us, and still is denied. Women deny it horribly with a grinning travesty of sex."[34]

The paintings were locked in a cell, and when the authorities threatened to destroy them, Lawrence agreed to get them out of England and never bring them back. He kept his word and the paintings managed to escape to Taos.

Saki Karavas, owner of La Fonda Hotel, and sometimes referred to as the Don Juan of Taos, was a serious art collector. The Taos Society of Artists, of which Kenneth Adams, friend of Susanna's mother, was the eighth member, met at the hotel regularly and exhibited their paintings in the lobby. When Frieda Lawrence died in 1956, she left part of her estate, including the Lawrence paintings, to her third husband, Angelino Ravagli. He sold them to Saki for an undisclosed price.

I was eager to view *The Forbidden Paintings*. The woman at the desk confirmed they were kept in a small locked room behind the reception. I paid my admission, she escorted me and unlocked the door.

I found the paintings a curious blend of kitsch and creepy with their recurrent theme of somehow deformed, small headed, fleshy mother-type women, and men with massive buttocks. The paintings did, however give me material for thought as I recalled the sex scenes in his novels.

Lawrence claimed that unlike the French and Italians, the English were artistically paralyzed by some old fear of sex, preferring to focus on landscapes rather than bodies. When they did venture into human subjects, they gave great attention to the details of clothing. No glorious nudes, no Michelangelo, no Degas.

Mind you, I couldn't help thinking, in that damp climate with its poorly heated, clammy country houses and a few weeks in summer when you could change into a bathing suit and shiver in the shallows at the beach, people were just not too fond of cavorting around nude, the way they might in sunny Italy or the south of France. Where would you even find a model in England prepared to lie around and freeze her butt? No wonder painters focused on clothing and those misty English landscapes! What about Lucien Freud's big fleshy nudes? Well, he was born in 1922, so by the time he hit his stride maybe his models could sprawl in front of the gas fire? Maybe.

Years ago, when my brother was at Oxford, David and I visited him and his wife. It was early autumn. The house was freezing and we'd take turns going downstairs to feed shillings to the gas meter so that we could eat dinner without shivering. Lying around nude was not high on our list of favorite activities.

Becoming Local

I began to imitate the local dress at Caffé Tazza; a long loosely pleated, "broomstick" skirt beneath which you could conceal according to the weather, appropriate layers of long underwear and tights; a colorful Guatemalan sweater over a tee shirt, and hiking boots equal to the mud. When I finally ventured out from Taos to Santa Fe, I gazed in wonder at the women in high heels walking on paved sidewalks.

From the beginning, I'd been forced to learn new skills. In Montreal if I needed gas, I'd simply drive down the hill to a full service gas station. When I looked for one in Taos I discovered that full service simply didn't exist. It was either self service or walk.

About three weeks after Adam left, I noticed my gas tank was running close to empty. I drove to the Chevron out on Pueblo del Sud and parked in front of the gas pump, got out of the car and took a look at all the machinery. It made me nervous. Finally I approached a large pick-up at the next pump. The back was filled with bales of straw and a huge black dog with a drooling mouth. I noticed the Colorado license plate.

The driver, a big guy with a beard had just finished filling his tank. What the heck, I'll probably never see him again, I thought and approached.

"Excuse me," I began. "I know you're going to wonder what planet

I just landed from but could you please show me how to fill my tank."

The guy looked at me for a moment to see if I was serious. Then he grinned. "Sure," he said. I paid close attention as he instructed me in the various buttons and levers. I was pathetically grateful. That day marked a significant level of achievement in my new life.

The House Next Door

On one side of my little house and *latilla* fenced garden, a colorful adobe wall painted with mermaids and angels concealed an unknown neighbor. On the other side, a tall fence separated me from the house next door closest to Mabel's, a house much newer than mine. Occasionally I heard a dog bark, and Bianca seemed interested as we passed the fence. Somebody had told me rather vaguely they thought a Baptist minister lived there, so one morning at Caffé Tazza, I was surprised when a woman asked whether I had met the woman next door "with all those big white dogs."

"The woman with the long blonde hair," she prompted. "I think she's Canadian and she has three dogs."

"You mean me? I only have one dog."

"No, I don't mean you." The woman gave me an odd look. "I mean the woman who looks like you who lives next door."

Late that afternoon I decided to investigate. With Bianca on her leash, I opened the gate next door and approached the front door. Sure enough, a woman of about my age, with similar long blonde hair opened the door amid the barking of a pack of large white wolfhounds. She looked as astonished as I felt.

The woman, whose name was Susan Bossenberry, invited us in. Borzoi always seem to welcome others of the breed and we turned them out to her backyard to meet and greet.

Susan was originally Canadian and had started Susan Wilder Fine Art, on the Plaza with partner, Rob Wilder. She was clearly as devoted to her three borzoi as I was to Bianca. The afternoon was sunny and we headed out into the yard, leaving the back door ajar.

Suddenly Susan jumped up and raced into the house. "I should check my dinner."

I heard a shriek. A moment later Bianca appeared. From her defiant expression I knew she'd been up to mischief. Susan appeared and shook her fist. "Your dog just ate my dinner," she said. "I had a nice little filet mignon on the grill and she took it right off the stove!" Fortunately Susan has a wonderful sense of humor.

We celebrated our meeting with a glass of nicely chilled chardonnay and I promised to take her to dinner at the Taos Inn to make up for my unmannerly cur. We and our four borzoi became fast friends after that, drifting in and out of each other's houses.

Susan's gallery welcomed many of the new young artists along with recognized landscape painters such as Stephen Day and Margaret Des. Later, when she moved the gallery to Kit Carson, it became the showcase for the huge paintings of Pueblo peoples by Rory Wagner. Browsing the many rambling rooms of the gallery offered a pleasant break from my writing. I looked forward to Susan's opening nights, she had the knack of making everyone feel welcome. Later, she hosted a book launch for me.

Susan knew everyone in town and was generous in her introductions. She invited me to meet her friend, Rhoda Blake over lunch at the Taos Inn. In 1954, Rhoda and her husband, Ernie, had seen their vision of a world class ski valley about twenty miles north of town. They moved on site with their three children in an eleven foot camper, which did not have power until 1963, and gradually created the lodge and trails which would become the world class Taos Ski Valley. Ernie died in 1989. I enjoyed chatting with Rhoda, one of the grand ladies of Taos, who would live a spirited life 'til her passing in 2013 at age 97.

Susan was also a friend of Frank Waters, one of Mabel's guests, who became known for his novel, *The Man Who Killed the Deer,* set in the

Taos Pueblo. Susan and her borzoi had stayed with Frank and his wife, Barbara, on their land in Arroyo Seco, north of town. One morning the two dogs escaped from the fenced yard. Borzoi are sight hounds and you quickly learn that they will take off at the speed of light if they spot a rabbit or anything else that moves.

"They got out and disappeared," Susan told me. "I was going out of my mind. What if they were hit by a car? Borzoi aren't road wise. A week went by and there was no news. Then about a week after that, someone phoned me over at Angel Fire. You know how many miles away that is? Twenty-four! Well she had both my borzoi. They'd wandered in for something to eat."

After our lunch with Rhoda Blake at the Taos Inn, I was eager to visit the Ski Valley. One day in the middle of winter, Susan called to invite me to accompany her up there to celebrate her friend, Barbara Cottam's birthday.

It was snowing lightly when we arrived in the Village and we admired the pretty snowflakes which drifted by the window. After a merry and lingering birthday lunch we headed out to play.

Susan, Barbara and their friend Cathy had arranged to have our photos taken on an old-fashioned sleigh, but by the time the four of us and Susan's borzoi, Kira, managed to pack ourselves onto the sleigh, a full-fledged snowstorm descended off the mountain in full swirl. As the big flakes covered our fuzzy rug, we were laughing so hard we almost fell off the sleigh.

As I settled into my new and healthy life on Morada Lane, it wasn't long before I began to imagine some changes to the house to bring in more light. The studio was fine as it was; in addition to the wall of sliding glass doors to the old apple tree, several large skylights flooded the room with sunshine. The previous owner had been a dancer and had installed a floor to ceiling mirror along one wall. All those windows made the studio a perfect, airy summer retreat, but with its one sputtering gas heater, a ubiquitous Taos variety, the room was a touch draughty and I'd learned to avoid draughts like the plague.

In the little house, I liked the dim, low-beamed feel of the kitchen and tiny sitting room but the two windows in the larger bedroom I used as an office and dining room, were small and high. It would, I decided, add to my enjoyment a great deal if I replaced them with a well-insulated wall of window on the garden. Mabel had written of watching the men of the Pueblo build the Big House from mud, straw and wood brought down from the hills.

I had no idea whether the Pueblo men still built houses in the town, but I was lucky to find the perfect carpenter, and fortunately he was available right away. I watched with great interest as Peter and his assistant removed the existing window then cut down into the thick walls to enlarge the opening, revealing old adobe bricks made of mud and straw. They had held up surprisingly well, but as they removed the bricks, the dust flew.

While the men chatted to me about the construction of the house, finally I understood why a fine covering of dust accumulated just days after I'd dusted and swept. The large wooden ceiling beams, or *vigas,* were flanked by smaller pieces of stripped sapling, *latillas*, then covered by a load of insulating earth before the flat roof was added. Mabel writes about a layer of sweet clover and sage which was added to the earth in the ceilings at the Big House. I had no idea whether they'd added clover and sage when they built my house, but it was clear that the packed earth released a steady film of dust.

Right in the middle of the construction, when the open wall to the garden was still covered with plastic, the weather changed dramatically. I went to bed with the house nice and warm from a bright sunny day which had heated the wraparound porch so that I could sit out there without a sweater. Next morning a coating of fluffy snow covered the ground. The house was cold. All those winters of bronchitis were deeply engraved in my memory from first the damp grey Melbourne winters, through the rainy winter David and I spent in Corfu and throughout my Montreal years. Now in Taos, I drank hot tea with lemon and honey, worried and waited. Nothing happened. By the time the new window was fully installed two days later, I was still ferociously healthy.

"It's working," I told my delighted husband. "This climate agrees with me."

It was a combination of the clean dry air and altitude, I believe. When my husband, David, and daughter, Tilke, visited me they'd spend time adjusting to the seven thousand foot altitude. For the first two days they felt tired and had headaches. Notices at the Taos Inn advised visitors to drink plenty of water to counteract these side effects. I was fortunate. The altitude seemed to agree with me and, like Mabel, I continued to experience a sense of heightened well-being.

The Count

By the time the new window was installed, and the linoleum in the same room replaced with warm, terracotta *saltillo* tiles, after luxuriating in front of the fire at Mabel's and at the Taos Book Shop, I wanted a fireplace. The antique woodstove with its gleaming polished silver top, was fine for heating but I wanted a hearth I could gaze into and watch the flames leap and crackle. One way or another it was, I decided, a serious omission.

When I mentioned this to the contractor who'd put in the window and floor, he said, "Oh, you need Steve Hinton. We call him The Count because he never works before noon."

Steve was a tall, slightly stooped, silver haired man with a certain elegance. In spite of his ski jacket and jeans, he looked as though he'd be more at home in a flowing velvet cloak. He studied my tiny sitting room. "What you need is a Rumford fireplace," he said. "You've heard of Rumford Baking Powder?" I nodded. "That's the man who invented the Rumford fireplace. Instead of sucking the heat up the chimney it will actually heat this room."

Over the next few weeks, Steve would arrive in the early afternoon. He selected the position for the fireplace after much consideration. Because of the glass door to the greenhouse, there wasn't much choice. Finally he decided that the best place was in the corner by the window, where I could sit facing it, looking into the kitchen. It would be a tight fit.

His work on the small raised corner fireplace was slow and painstaking. He enjoyed chatting as he worked. He'd lived in Mexico City and now had settled up in the mountains in St. Christobal at the Lama Foundation, a Buddhist community. His aunt had been an innovative educator; she'd helped start The Putney School in Vermont and the Verde Valley School in Sedona, Arizona.

He stopped work at four and joined me for tea. I was sorry when the fireplace was complete. I'd enjoyed his company and our tea-time chats.

Bianca and I drove down the highway to Ranchos de Taos, where all the woodpiles lined the road, and filled the trunk of the Explorer with firewood. The Count had been right. The small raised Rumford fireplace easily warmed the room and I loved the smell of the *piñon* firewood when Bianca and I walked outside before bed to admire the stars.

Now I could spend my evenings reading in front of my own hearth. I got hold of Miriam Hapgood Dewitt's, *Taos, a Memory*. Miriam was the daughter of Greenwich Village writers, Hutchins Hapgood and Neith Boyce, those writer friends of Mabel's she hung out with in Provincetown. Miriam had succumbed to the malady which seemed epidemic for young women breaking free of the old order: depression. Following a prolonged bout, Taos offered twenty-three-year-old Miriam, the escape proven effective by a steady stream of young women.

She went out with her brother, Charles and her mother, Neith, in the summer of 1929. Charles, in his first letter home to his father, wrote, "This country seems to me like the other side of the moon, nature being so different from anything I have ever imagined before, that the similarities to my former way of living stand out in isolation, like a few scattered known words in a strange language."[35]

Miriam's mother, however, couldn't wait to return east. Her children saw beauty and romance, she saw "poverty and disease and danger." She was unwell and a nest of rattlesnakes discovered under her doorstep did not add to her enjoyment.

Later, when their mother returned east, Mabel took young Miriam and her brother, Charles, under her wing, accompanying them on horseback excursions into the mountains. Miriam wrote,

"Mabel sits her horse well. She is stocky, her black hair cut in a bang like the Indian women, a scarf around her head. At this period of her life, her face and figure are undistinguished and she wears simple dresses with gathered skirts. But her extraordinary eyes, hazel and thickly lashed, her deep beautifully modulated voice and her self-assurance set her apart. They demand attention and respect. Yet it is difficult to explain her power. She has a mysterious power to attract, to stimulate, to bring people together."[36]

Summer of 1929

After I pieced together the relationships, I began to imagine the summer of 1929, up at Mabel's. Georgia O'Keeffe and her friend Rebecca Strand (Beck) were staying in the Pink House. Both wore black skirts and white shirts. Beck wore a black Stetson. She was painting "exquisite flowers on glass." Brett was there in her customary baggy velveteen pants and boots, a belted beaded vest, a Stetson and a hearing trumpet she'd christened, Toby. Painter, John Marin, who'd create a large body of watercolors while in Taos, was also visiting.

Writer Spud Johnson, editor of *The Laughing Horse*, in defiance of Prohibition, mixed Taos Lightnings, orange juice and raw corn whiskey. Young Miriam Hapgood, her brother Charles and their mother, Neith, also hung out in the courtyard. Add Ella Young, Irish mystic and writer, for good measure. Bees buzzed over the big central bed of pink and white and red hollyhocks.

That was the summer the police raided the London gallery and seized the *Forbidden Paintings*. The Lawrences were in France, D. H. suffering from the tuberculosis which would claim his life the following year.

Mabel had gone back to Buffalo for a hysterectomy; her doctor had diagnosed uterine fibroids. Having had my appendix removed when I was eighteen, I could imagine how she felt bumping up on that road through the Rio Grande Gorge to Taos. I could not, however, imagine how she felt when she returned home and the house was packed with guests.

O'Keeffe had sent voluminous letters to Mabel describing how charming Tony had been, driving her around the countryside. Was that of much comfort to Mabel?

Neith Boyce wrote to her husband, "Everything is upset since Mabel got back and everyone quarreling! She of course isn't feeling well and is nervous and irritable."[37] No kidding! Shortly after her return to Taos, Mabel overdid things, developed heart problems and was driven down to the hospital in Albuquerque.

As I imagined the partying that swirled around her, I concluded that Mabel was a saint to put up with all those guests!

Another incident topped off that summer; the murder of Arthur Manby, the eccentric Englishman with whom Mabel, her son, John, and Maurice had stayed on their arrival in Taos. Manby was involved in all kinds of wheeling, dealing and land acquisition and was disliked by more than a few. He was discovered in his house, his head cut off. His two guard dogs had been gnawing on the grisly remains.

I wondered what Ella Young, the Irish mystic, had to say about that very odd, off-balance summer. Did she interpret the events as harbingers of the The Crash which would wreak havoc with the market that fall?

The Lawrence Women

Somehow, as I went through my pile of books, all roads led to D. H. Lawrence, so I began with Mabel's, *Lorenzo in Taos*. Years before that fateful summer of 1929, she read his book, *Sea and Sardinia*, and she decided that D. H. was uniquely qualified to truly appreciate the New Mexican landscape. "He gives the feel and touch and smell of places so that their reality and their essence are open to one, and one can see right into them."[38] She sent a letter inviting him and Frieda to Taos, but they dragged their heels and first finished up in Australia where he wrote his novel, *Kangaroo*.

Leo Stein, art critic brother of Gertrude, who had attended Mabel's Florence salons, had also visited her in Taos. He claimed that the vistas behind the sacred mountain surpassed any of the great Chinese landscapes. "No landscape I have ever seen elsewhere," he wrote to Lawrence, "is as beautiful."[39] He also urged D. H. to accept Mabel's invitation. He said of her, "Mabel Sterne is the all but perfect hostess. She'll take you everywhere and show you everything. She has immense energy, and capacity to make things happen without any irritating restlessness. She's a kind of reposeful hurricane. She is completely at home in New Mexico, and is the only educated, cultivated woman that I know of who has broken through the barrier between red and white and keeps it open in both directions. Incidentally, Mabel is not a lion hunter. She's been used to lions all her life and is quite some little lioness herself. But she is a delightful and appreciative companion, and at Taos you can have society or solitude in such measure and forms as you prefer."[40]

The Lawrences arrived in Taos, on his 37th birthday, September 11, 1922. That evening was not auspicious. When they arrived at the Big House he was tired and cranky. They sat down to dinner. D. H. said of the dining room "It's like one of those nasty little temples in India." Not exactly a gracious way to endear yourself to your hostess, but Mabel, with saintly tolerance, continued to shower him and Frieda with her generosity. Fortunately he felt about the land as she had hoped.

"In the magnificent fierce morning of New Mexico," he wrote, "one sprang awake. A new part of the soul woke up suddenly and the old world gave way to the new."[41]

The Lawrences stayed in the Two Story House. Blonde, voluptuous, Frieda, was enthusiastic about living to the full. She and Mabel discovered they had much in common. Frieda was born also in luxury, a Prussian baroness, in 1879, the same year as Mabel. The two women became mothers in 1902. Both were patrons of the arts and moved with the most creative minds of the time.

After an unfulfilling marriage and three children, Frieda met Lawrence and left her son with his father, her two daughters with her parents. The separation triggered years of suffering for her children and for herself, as their father prevented them from seeing her for many years.

D. H. was dependent on Frieda. She was his "love goddess," at home in her body. He believed that "man gets his power from a woman." That may have been so, but he did not always treat her well. Rachel Hawk, who rented a cabin to the Lawrences at one point, witnessed a violent and brutal temper. When this erupted, Hawk observed that he'd beat up on a horse, or tie his dog up and beat it and if they weren't around he would beat up on Frieda. At one point Mabel, soaking in one of the nearby hot springs, noticed that Frieda's white body was covered with black and blue bruises.

Somehow he remained a literary god to both women, who were somehow prepared to overlook such cruelty. Inevitably, they locked horns as they vied for his attention. D. H. showed some interest in Mabel's writing process and she was grateful for his opinions and criticisms, which did not always serve her well.

She wrote him of her "uneasiness in action." "The thing that releases me from this gummed-up state is writing. If I can overcome the terrible resistance and inertia that seizes me before I begin—if I can once get started and know I want to say something—it comes. Then I am off—in a good running pace. And after having done some writing, everything is different. The room I sit in seems beneficent, and the light bathes one in a mild, peaceful glow. All the misery and tug and pull are gone. Living isn't a mess and a struggle, and the beating blood inside doesn't beat at one anymore. It goes along like a river at the same tempo as the sun."[42]

Perhaps one factor which contributed to her difficulty getting started, was Lawrence's remark to her, "I shall never consider you a writer or even a knower." These arrogant words paralyzed her, creating still more inertia to overcome. In another letter. He tells her, "You haven't enough restraint in you for creative writing, but you can make a document. Only don't go at it too slap-dash—makes it unreal."[43]

In her letters to Lawrence, Mabel demonstrates an incongruous lack of self-confidence, also created in her by her psychoanalyst A. A. Brill. Was it a symptom of the times that the strongest of talented women still saw themselves reflected only in the approval of men?

Mabel's son, John, did not care for the Lawrences. He told friends, "Mother is tired of those Lawrences always sponging on her." Word got back to the them and they left in a huff and rented a cabin on the Hawk Ranch. When all the drama receded, Mabel offered them the 160 acre Lobo ranch, twenty miles north of Taos. D. H., claiming contempt for possessions, wanted the deed put only in Frieda's name and she, not wanting a handout, insisted Mabel take the manuscript to *Sons and Lovers* in exchange.

Things settled into some sort of peace. The Lawrences and Mabel visited each other at the ranch and at the Big House. D. H. spent only two years at the ranch before a return to Europe and his death in Vence, France in 1930. One of his letters to Mabel from Austria, three years before his death amused me. "Heard from Brett today—she says you are learning to drive the Buick and stepping on the gas like ten heroines.

Don't do it. Stepping on the gas one goes over the edge, which is not an arrival."[44]

His last letter, sent from Vence, France, just before his death, is a sudden departure from former criticisms and advice. Finally he offers the kindness she craved, as he urges her to "try to give up yourself, try to yield yourself entirely to your body, and let it take its own life at last. You have bullied it so much, even to having your womb removed. Now try to love it, to think tenderly of it, and let it come to its own life at last. Lie still and gradually let your body come to its own life, free at last of our will—if we can manage it, and I can come to New Mexico, then we can begin a new life, with real tenderness in it."[45]

After his death Frieda returned to Taos, later marrying Italian, Angelino Ravagli. As they grew older, Mabel and Frieda became close friends, along with London painter, Dorothy Brett whom D.H. had invited to Taos when he and Frieda returned to Mabel's for the second time. Brett, like Mabel and Frieda appears to have been happy to serve Lawrence in return for his company.

I finished my exploration of what Saki at the Hotel La Fonda described as "the Lawrence women" by reading Brett's book, *Lawrence and Brett*.

The Honorable Dorothy Brett was the daughter of Viscount Escher. Both her parents had a place in the courts of Victoria and then Edward; Brett and her sister lived a sheltered childhood and attended dancing classes at Buckingham Palace. When she was around fourteen, a family acquaintance frightened her with his lewd advance, but it was said that Brett remained ignorant to the facts of life until she was thirty.

When she decided to study at London's Slade School of Art, she set out to establish herself as a painter and her own person. She invited her circle of artists and writers to her tiny rooms off Earl's Court, and on one of these occasions, Lawrence came by. Lawrence, eager to have friends with him in Taos, invited her. When he and Frieda made the trip to Taos for the second time, in 1923, Brett accompanied them.

Of meeting Mabel for the first time, Brett wrote, "She is shorter than I am, of a square, sturdy build; the thick hair, bobbed like a

Florentine boy, swings as she walks and gleams here and there a bright chestnut. The big, gray, dark-lashed eyes are curiously shiny, the nose small and straight, with just the least bit of a curve down at the end. The lips are well cut and unpainted. There is poise and self-assurance in the whole carriage, and a warm glow from what one feels in a moment is a rich personality. As she walks, her arms swing and some of the force and strength lying behind the charm reveals itself."[46]

From her arrival in Taos, until Lawrence's death, Brett maintained a devoted friendship with D. H., as she helped clean up and repair the cabins on the Kiowa Ranch, type his manuscripts and accompany him on walks. When Frieda implied that their relationship was physical, Brett responded, "But Frieda, how can I make love with Lawrence when I am your guest? Would that not be rather indecent?"

Frieda replied, "Lawrence says he could not possibly be in love with a woman like you—an asparagus stick."[47] Brett appeared to have been an expert at friendliness, it oozed from her, and before long, she and Frieda were roaring with laughter.

Brett liked to venture out into the land and spent time on horseback with her friend, Betty Cottam, also a friend of Mabel's. Much of the time, Brett worked to lift Lawrence's flagging spirits. She described a picnic at Manby Hot Springs. D. H., Frieda and Brett joined Betty Cottam in her car. Brett wrote, "By the time I come out of the spring, out of that dark, mysterious, uncanny water, like a black opal,...you're feeling low, no animation, no spirit. You and Frieda go into the spring while Betty and I spread the lunch out on the warm rocks.

"As we drive home, you say the bathing has done you good, that you feel more lively, more impudent."[48]

After Lawrence's death, Brett returned to her small cabin on the Hawk ranch, that she dubbed The Tower Beyond Tragedy, where her English sheepdog, Balliol kept her company. She wrote in her memoirs about Lawrence, "I could go on writing of you forever."

In spite of clashes among Frieda, Brett and Mabel, they enjoyed many light-hearted times, with frequent outings on horseback, picnicking up in the hills, enjoying the pristine landscape. When the Lawrences moved into the Kiowa Ranch, Brett moved into the tiny shack my friend Susanna, had mentioned when she described her mother's invitation to the ranch for tea in 1924. The shack was uninhabitable in winter and Brett descended to Mabel's as the weather grew cold.

She was a free-spirit and something of a vagabond. At one point, Susan-next-door told me, Brett moved north of town and shared an outhouse with writer, Frank Waters.

Before finally settling into the house where she would live until her death at ninety-three, now The Brett House restaurant, north of the former "Blinking Light" on the way to the Ski Valley, she moved down to Mabel's and painted in the same studio that O'Keeffe would use that summer of 1929, the one near the Two-Story House.

When I had finished reading about the three women, I studied a photo of Mabel, Frieda and Brett. They look a strong-willed and jolly trio. A cigarette sticks straight out from Frieda's mouth. They had started out rivals for D. H.'s attention, then over the years had become best friends. I couldn't help thinking about the sad way women traditionally have been pitted against each other to vie for the attention of men. Fortunately, for the most part, we've finally managed to shake off these old male-centered restraints and enjoy the full bounty of friendship with other women.

In *Winter in Taos*, when Brett is away, Mabel writes, "Brett is somewhere in a room I don't know, talking with people I have never seen, painting a portrait I may never see. This seems strange to me, because we have been so much together for ten years and I am always able to visualize her in the places where she goes, for they have been familiar to me. Her letter had new strange names in it and I felt as though she had got away from me!"

"Frieda, too, writing from far away, of curious new fruits and lovely embroideries, seemed to me away on another planet, for the winter isolation bore down on me this night and I couldn't overcome the sense of emptiness and silence that kept returning to confound me." She missed Frieda's "zestfulness and warm exuberance."

Fortunately Mabel enjoyed the simple delights of food. I found this endearing.

"Supper was comforting, though. Hot cocoa and a chop and warm soda biscuits, crisp lettuce with a great deal of garlic flavoring with Italian oil, cheese and crackers and a piece of cold pumpkin pie!"[49]

Yummy! By now, I had spent so much time reading about each of these three women, sitting down to meals with them, listening to their conversations, that Mabel, Frieda and Brett were beginning to feel like my own friends.

Remembering Mabel: Lunch With Phoebe Cottam

A few mornings after my first walk to Mabel's with Bianca, a pack of barking dogs approached us. I froze, apprehensive, as Bianca, a swift flash of silvery white, pulled her leash free from my hand and took off after the pack. Borzoi had been bred in Russia to chase wolves and hold them down until the hunters arrived. Clearly it was bred in the bone, for the pack fled, tails between their legs. That was the last time we saw them. Later I would learn about Mabel's pack of dogs from Phoebe Cottam.

By now I had read volumes by and about Mabel and her friends. The definitive work was the meticulously researched, *New Woman, New World*, by Lois Palken Rudnick to which I'd return many times. I loved her details. However, I had not met anyone who had actually known Mabel.

Mabel had died in 1962 at age eighty-three. Now, thirty years later, my chances of meeting anyone who'd known her were rather slim, so I was thrilled when Susan-next-door told me about Phoebe Cottam. We were sitting in my kitchen over a glass of white wine, our borzoi lounging on the lawn.

"You know, you're a writer, you're interested in Mabel," Susan told me, "You live in one of her little houses, you should talk to Phoebe Cottam, her husband ran Cottam's Ford in town. She and her husband were good friends of Mabel's. They actually lived in her Big House when Mabel and Tony moved across the lane. They knew Brett and Frieda too."

Some time later I finally met Phoebe Cottam when Susan invited me to one of her parties.

A few weeks later, I was excited when Susan suggested we get together for lunch with Phoebe. We met at Doc Martin's Restaurant at The Taos Inn, not far from where Arthur Manby, whose head was severed, summer of 1929, had lived. Our table was set down a few stairs in a sunny alcove with a view of the patio, where a table of skiers were sunning themselves.

Phoebe was an elegantly dressed woman in a black woolen jacket with a southwest motif. As we greeted each other she radiated warmth and friendliness. She ordered a martini. I asked how she had come to Taos.

"I was born in Santa Fe," she began. "My dad had a car dealership in Texas and all the dealerships were going broke so they moved to Santa Fe and he ran a dealership there. We lived all the way at the top of Canyon Road, right up there near what's now the Bird Sanctuary, up past El Christo Rey Church. We lived up past that on the ridge. There were three army colonels who lived up there.

"My parents had two daughters and they didn't want children up there but we were very well behaved. I had a little sister, we were very close but she died when she was very young. Then I had a baby sister. She came late, just before we left Santa Fe. I loved Santa Fe. I knew who lived in every house on Palace Avenue. It doesn't feel like I've been gone that long.

"Next door to us was Colonel Andy and there was a gate in the high wall between our properties and my parents said never go through that gate so of course we did, and the gate closed and I couldn't get back. So I went to Mrs. Andy's house and knocked and she was really an old bag and she said, well, you'll just have to get out any way you can. I was about eight years old, so it was too high to climb over, there was no way, so I yelled and our housekeeper heard me and let me out and I never went over there again."

"In forty-four, we came up here to Taos and my dad started his own dealership. My husband, Brooke, and I met when I was twelve or thirteen and he was thirteen, maybe fourteen and there was a guest ranch owned by a friend of ours. They knew I liked to ride, so they invited me to come ride with them. They had three or four guests and

89

Brooke was there. After that we were good friends during the holidays. The rest of the time I was away at school in San Antonio.

"There weren't many Anglos here in Taos back then. When we had a party we'd have all the Anglos, maybe twenty or thirty people. There were artists who lived here just in the summer. We were all very social. We had a lot of culture; there was a theater, a wooden building where the TCA (Taos Community Center) is now. The old one burned down.

"It was fun because everyone in Taos would take part in the plays. All of us were very good friends. I was the youngest in the group. There were very few children. Artists didn't have children, so we few were very spoiled. We had parties all the time, once a week.

" After I finished school, Brooke and I were married, but he was in the army, so I continued to live at home until after the war was over. Mabel was a friend of Brooke's mother, Betty Cottam," said Phoebe, "so she said why don't we come and stay in one of her houses, she had a whole complex of houses and she used to invite people to stay.

"Mabel had five dogs," Phoebe told us as she sipped her martini. "My parents didn't have dogs, so I didn't know much about them. She had these two little bulldogs and two Dalmations and a big basset hound and we'd bought a little Sealyham terrier. Well, she came into season and Mabel's pack came after her. We were upstairs in the Two-Story House and the dogs came up the outdoor staircase. The little Sealyham was fine, she defended herself, but I had to carry each of Mabel's five dogs down the stairs. Oh my!

"Mabel was sooo nice to us. She was just thrilled to have us. She and Tony came to see us every morning. At first I was offended because they'd drive up and honk. My mother had told me don't ever go out with anyone who honks. But Tony was getting older then, so they'd honk, and he'd get out and come to the door.

"The Two Story House was Mabel's first house, across the field. It was impossible, nobody had taken care of it at all, so I decided to turn it over. I proceeded to paint the trim white instead of an ugly green. Mabel said I was the only one who had ever gotten the cobwebs down. People stayed there for a while, they didn't care. She had the St. Theresa House, and the gatehouse and the studio.

"So we all lived up there and then the maids had a little house. Mabel and Tony had just built a new house across Morada Lane and the Big House was empty. Her son, John, would come every now and then. By then she thought the house was too big, it was huge. We lived in the Two Story House for eight years. When we moved there we already had our first son, John Brooke and we had three more sons there.

"And Mabel said, come live in my Big House 'cos it's empty. The Big House was wonderful because it had central heat and everything worked and we had her gardeners. Back then the garden looked just like it does now. The dovecotes were there with live pigeons."

Phoebe paused, then chuckled. "Our little boys were so bad, they'd go out and shoot at them. We used the whole house. Brooke and I were upstairs and there are four bedrooms downstairs. Brett had painted the bathroom upstairs, the one with the painted windows."

"When I first arrived someone told me D. H. Lawrence had painted those windows," I said. Phoebe shook her head. "No, it was Brett. The house was very comfortable. We lived there for two years, until Mabel's death.

"You know, there are all sorts of stories about Mabel being difficult but we didn't see that at all, because by that time she had mellowed and she loved Brooke, my husband. We had the Ford dealership downtown. Tony and Mabel would visit Brooke there, then Mabel would go home and have lunch. Tony would get restless and he'd go and pick up his friend the gardener and they'd drive around all afternoon in the car and Mabel would get antsy.

"Before we moved into the Big House, my son, John Brooke, he was around two, and I would go over to Mabel's around four-thirty and we'd drink bourbon. Mabel was good fun and she loved John Brooke. He would always sit on her lap. I can still see it, and one day, Brett , she was always there, said, I hope you're not giving that baby any of your drink, Mabel. John Brooke got very rambunctious and Brett said, my goodness, I think she is. I don't think he remembers at all but Frieda and Mabel and Brett all doted on him.

"After a while I'd have to go, I couldn't just stay there all afternoon,

I had things to do. Mabel would say, Brett, I'm tired of you now, go home and Brett would go. I thought it was terrible the way Mabel talked to her. She never talked that way to me. She would get anxious about Tony out running around and they probably had a bottle of whiskey in the car. She'd call Brooke at the dealership and say have you seen Tony and usually he had and she'd say, well I wish you'd go get him and bring him home and he would."

Phoebe thought for a while, then she said, "Everyone we really knew all those years is dead, even all the help. The ladies who worked for Mabel, two darling ladies, Raphaelita and Isobel. They cooked. Just plain old food. We used to eat there a lot with Tony and Mabel. Tony had lovely manners. After dinner he'd say, thank you very much, very nice meal and then he'd go in his room and play the drums. In their new house there was a long hall and bedrooms on each side and if you kept walking, she had a big living room and to the left was the little kitchen. The house didn't feel like the Big House but it felt like Mabel. I always felt so at home there. She always had fresh flowers, whatever was around, I remember the daffodils.

"I thought she was dowdy. She wore baggy dresses and she liked pink. She always wanted me to get dressed for dinner and she bought me party dresses. I changed from my shorts but I didn't get that dressed up. I'd put on other clothes but not one of those long dresses she bought me. I still have lots of those dresses. Long dresses with scooped necks. She liked me in yellow. My mother and Mabel had a sort of tug of war over me. Mother would call Mabel and say I've been trying to find Phoebe all morning, is she there? Mabel would say yes and Mother would say, well, I wish she'd stay home.

"It's amazing that she liked me because she fought with everyone else. I think she liked me because I was so young and naïve. When we lived at the Two Story House it kind of got on her nerves that I wanted to get everything straightened up. If she didn't like what I did she'd send Max, her groundsman over. He was a darling man. Mabel was very picky, she kept everything very neat. The lilacs were always trimmed and they took care of the road.

"I missed all that time when Mabel had guests because I was still a teenager. Georgia O'Keeffe came and I met her. She didn't like children. Millicent Rogers came and lived up there in the Tony house. She and Mabel just didn't get along at all. Mabel had a lot of parties and Millicent had a lot of parties and they tried to outdo each other. I was still in high school and I wasn't that aware of it. They were just the grown-ups to me. Later, after Brooke and I were married, Mabel still had parties. She loved them, music and food and she liked to get in an eyelock, mostly with the men.

"Bonnie, Mabel's granddaughter and she didn't get along at all. I think it was a personality thing. She had a brother, Sammy. We did a lot together. Bonnie was about five years younger than I am and Sammy a couple of years younger than Bonnie. Bonnie was John's daughter by his second wife. His first wife was "little Alice." She was the daughter of the poet from Santa Fe, Alice Corbin. The marriage wasn't good but they had three daughters. The only one alive now is Tish."

Our grilled salmon arrived. Phoebe finished her martini. "When we were at the Big House we had parties all the time. All that beautiful furniture was there, it was French provincial and aqua. In the little hall when you walked in was a day bed and some books. We used the Rainbow Room as a family room and that aqua French furniture was in there. Then we turned it into a music room and when we had parties we'd end up in there because the living room wasn't very cozy. There was a big aqua sofa and a desk and a darling old corner fireplace and a yellow chair where Mabel always sat. There wasn't a lot of furniture. I think she took a lot to her new house across Morada Lane.

"Dennis Hopper comes to Taos occasionally and when I see him again I'll ask him about the furniture. Last time I saw him, we were right here at the Taos Inn and I wanted to get up and say something but my children wouldn't let me so I didn't say a word but it makes me mad that he took it. There's none of her furniture there now. I go over occasionally and it looks very nice. She had lovely sconces and doors. We'd sit out over the *acequia* but the water isn't running anymore, we just haven't had much water, but some year we will. It was wonderful there and the children loved it. It was nice to have all that space.

"She had a corral down below with two men who worked all the time, Indians who were Tony's cousins. They kept everything in order."

As we were waiting for our apple-pear croustade, Phoebe said, "You know, we had a different experience with Mabel than a lot of the artists and writers who'd stay there, she would just get bored and impatient with them and the Lawrences just got tired of her bossing them around so they went to live up at St. Christobal. D. H. died in 1930 and we moved out of the Two-Story House to the Big House in nineteen sixty.

"I knew Frieda really well. I loved Frieda. I was just sixteen when she came here. My parents were very conservative. Frieda and her second husband, Angie, got me my first horse and we spent a lot of time at her house. I can't believe how we got around in the snow on our horses.

"Angie, his name was Angelino, was a potter, he had a wheel and we were there a lot. Frieda would have open house on Sundays. At her new house right behind what's now Conoco. She lived to make cookies. She'd give us grapefruit juice with water. She had a wonderful German voice. It was very entertaining.

"I didn't know that she had left her children for D. H. I was horrified. She loved children, but I guess she and Lawrence just had an eyelock and she went with him and left those three kids.

"I found out about what happened when I went to school and I was shocked. Then I read all the books. I knew Brett well too. She and Mabel had a wonderful time fighting. They fought about everything. Mabel would say, be quiet, Brett, nobody's talking to you. Brett was a very dear friend also. My mother-in-law had known all those girls forever. Brooke's uncle had a ranch right next to the Lawrence Ranch. They didn't like Lawrence much but Brett and Mabel adored him. Mabel could handle anyone and they were always together, you know.

"Frieda died in fifty-six, Mabel died in sixty-two. Brett died in seventy-seven in her house on the corner near the Blinking Light where the Brett House Restaurant is now.

"The relationship between Mabel and Tony was darling, they were very close. I'd read how when she came here she met him and I was amazed that she was attracted to him."

We lingered over coffee. Susan and I saw Phoebe to her car. Then we walked up Morada Lane. "You know I often imagine how it must have been up at Mabel's," said Susan. "It would have been so much fun to have been in Taos at that time. Sometimes I think we live in the past here. I wonder how people will think about the artists who show in my gallery a hundred years from now."

That night I sat in my little greenhouse. It had been a glorious warm day and the glass walls still held the heat. I watched a crescent moon rise behind the hills and I thought about Phoebe and Brooke and her mischievous little boys and that vibrant time in Taos that now felt so alive to me.

Tea at Phoebe's

Some time later, Phoebe invited me to visit her at home for tea, out past the local marker, the "Blinking Light" at the intersection of the road to the Ski Valley and the back roads that wound through the back country and up into Colorado. We sat in the comfortable living room, where several of Brett's paintings hung. As we sipped our tea, her Doberman watched us from the doorway.

"We moved out to this house in sixty-three," Phoebe told me, "the year after Mabel died and that's when we stopped riding our horses everywhere. When we were children there really wasn't much to do except ride our horses. We'd swim at the Ponce de Leon spring.

"When all the hippies came to town in the sixties my boys were getting bigger and I was so busy. Dennis Hopper bought Mabel's. He turned it into a commune, I think. He was quite under the influence. I really didn't see him that much. After Dennis left, the house needed work and several people bought Mabel's. I didn't really know them. Now they use it for a cultural center. Bob Atire owns it now, he has wonderful folks in there running it. He did very good work when he restored the house and it looks just the way it used to. I love to go there now. It always feels magical. "

Caffè Tazza

Unlike Montreal, where David and I often went out at night, my new social life, other than a meal or two with Susanna or Susan-next-door, occurred mostly in daylight. When there was a lull between workshops at Mabel's, I'd call in and chat with Maria. Around eleven, when I finished my morning's writing, I'd walk down to Caffè Tazza on Kit Carson, that local institution which reflected its hippie roots from the late sixties and the seventies when Dennis Hopper, of *Easy Rider* fame, bought Mabel's.

My conversations at Caffè Tazza revealed fascinating details about Taos. "Did you know that if you were to take a globe of the world and run a long pin through from Taos, it would come out in Tibet? Maybe that explains why Tibetan refugees are attracted to Taos." I learned that during Dennis Hopper's reign up at Mabel's, he had dubbed the house the Mud Palace. He tried to heat each room with a wood burning stove. Then he rented them out and when he put the house up for sale, that would be around seventy-six, when the realtors showed the property, these nude hippies were wandering around everywhere. You live up there near Mabel's? I wish I'd been there when Dennis Hopper had the place. Did you know Bob Dylan and Leonard Cohen, all the heavies, came to visit?"

The locals at Caffè Tazza made frequent references to "Taos Time."

"The plumber was supposed to come out this morning," a woman told me. "I waited and waited for him. Then I just gave up." She shrugged. "I guess he was on Taos Time."

Once, when I went into Moby Dickens Bookstore on the corner

of Bent Street and the John Dunn Plaza, I selected a book. There was nobody around. I waited patiently, then knocked respectfully on the counter. A woman with her hair tumbling out of a bun appeared around a bookshelf. When she saw I had a book to buy she gave me a withering look. "I can't sell you anything now. The toilet's overflowing." She turned her back and disappeared into the back of the store. I had been puzzled until I heard of Taos Time.

Several times a month, the large room at Tazza, the one with all the big red geraniums, was packed for readings by local writers and poets. Sometimes I'd see John Nichols. Susanna told me they sold a lot of his book, *The Milagra Beanfield Wars*. "Poor John, he came into the bookstore once and bumped his head on the low doorway. I think he saw stars. We took him inside and sat him down. Oh dear."

I looked forward to readings at Tazza. They were fun and after a day of my own writing, I was happy to hear the work of others.

My first week in Taos, Adam and I had gone to Dancing For Andrea, at the Taos Inn. Andrea was a local artist who'd needed surgery and this was a fund-raiser. We watched couples raise the dust with a two-step, and crowds lined up at the silent auction table.

"I guess Andrea's pretty popular," I remarked to a woman beside me.

"Oh no, Andrea's very shy."

Calling All Angels

One morning as I was reading *The Taos News*, a small ad. "*Calling All Angels*," grabbed my attention. Angels, with those wonderful big wings, have always fascinated me. Appearing out of the blue to perform miracles! Mabel had written in a letter to a friend, "There is no news. Only the miracles that occur each day."

What were you supposed to wear to meet an angel? The nights had been growing warmer and I settled on a long winter-white knitted dress. At 6:40 I climbed into my Explorer, Bianca, as usual standing on the back seat equally eager for adventure.

"We're having night life," I told her and her dark brown eyes sparkled. Bianca loved nightlife. Back in Montreal she'd often accompany me to parties where she'd beg shamelessly. People were delighted to indulge her and her favorite delicacy was lobster.

It was already dark and I'd never driven into the maze of narrow streets below the Plaza. By the time I found the small adobe house it was seven minutes past seven.

The front room was dimly lit with a flickering light, probably from candles, the windows covered by filmy white curtains. I parked the car behind a row of seemingly quite ordinary vehicles. Did they belong to contemporary angels or simply neighbors?

Bianca scanned the surrounds with customary vigilance, then settled into her patrol position on the back seat.

I smoothed my long white woolen dress and made my way up the front path. Reluctant to disturb the angels, instead of approaching the closed front door I noticed that the patio door of the lighted room was open. Perhaps I could just slip in without disturbing the heavenly throng.

As I pushed aside the white curtain, a light breeze ruffled my hair. Suddenly a room full of women faced me, staring as though they'd seen a ghost. I mumbled my apologies and scuttled to an empty chair as quickly as I could. There was a silence. Finally the leader continued to discuss the qualities of angels and how we mortals might develop similar ones.

Later, when we were drinking lemonade and munching brownies in the kitchen, one of them told me, "Our leader had just told us, 'I have a feeling we'll see an angel tonight,' and just then the curtain fluttered and you appeared in your long white dress. You were all backlit and with your long hair, for a moment I thought, it's really happening."

Though I enjoyed meeting a group of women who turned out to be dedicated to the needs of the community, I'd somehow expected something more ethereal. This was, after all, the home of the Sacred Mountain. By now I'd been told at least ten times, "The Mountain chooses you or it doesn't. If it likes you, you get to stay and have a good experience. If not, things go bad and it spits you out."

So far, the Mountain had been kind to me. I was ferociously healthy, not even a sniffle or cough. The little house was shaping up, I was friends with Susanna and with Susan-next-door and my writing was progressing smoothly. I'd decided to mine my experiences with illness for a new novel.

Set in Montreal in winter, *The Loneliness of Angels* was coming along nicely. During my years of illness I'd explored many different alternative cures that would have delighted my new friends at Caffé Tazza. Now, these yielded material I needed as I watched my characters move into place; a group of people all with life-threatening illnesses.

In The New Morning Healing Center, cures revolve around the Ann Wigmore diet of living foods, sprouted seeds, wheatgrass juice and a drink called Rejuvelac, made from fermented wheat berries. In my efforts to combat winter illness, I had firsthand experience of each of these. I had taken a large bottle of Rejuvelac with me to Bennington and kept it in the communal fridge. Unfortunately it smelled like vomit. My fellow students complained loudly until I told them it was a very potent fermented brew. I hoped this would create a more worldly profile than an enzymatic healing tonic.

Sitting at my desk in Taos, that faraway winter world of Montreal began to bring words to the page as I listened to the characters and felt for them as they clung together and tried to cope with the icy blasts, the blizzards and their fears of dying.

I included information about colonic irrigations, part of the detox program offered at The New Morning Center.

This was before colonics had become fashionable in progressive places like Santa Barbara and Santa Fe. When my French Canadian agent sent the book to New York she phoned me. "They were screaming at me that your book was obscene! You can hack someone to death with a chain saw, you can include incest and rape, any form of murder, but do not, absolutely do not mention a colon!"

Fortunately the French found cleansing the colon practical and very sensible and it was translated to *La Solitude des Anges*, shortly after its publication in English.

I was intrigued to learn that Mabel had also been interested in alternative approaches to healing and had explored a whole range of them for the challenges of her own health. Somehow this information strengthened my growing sense of Mabel as a kindred spirit.

The End of the Universe Café: Salted Peanuts

Out of the blue, the Mountain threw me a puzzling experience. I'd just started Wednesday morning yoga classes in the arts building set back from the road beside the Taos Inn. The weather had turned cold again. It had snowed the previous night, and as I left the class and crossed the small courtyard behind an adobe wall, I was bundled up head to toe in my shapeless down-stuffed coat.

She was sitting on a bench against the wall, wearing a short plaid skirt, and a navy twin-set. Her straight dark hair was chin length and her eyes a very dark blue.

"Hello," she said. "My name is Sal."

"I'm Valmai," I returned her greeting. Instead of an expected exchange of pleasantries, she said abruptly. "There are two of us. Would Valmai like to have tea with us today at The End of the Universe Café?" I'd heard the place had just opened off the plaza.

Still eager to make friends, I readily agreed, assuming she had a sister or friend. At four o'clock I climbed the outside stairs of one of the buildings on Paseo de Pueblo Norte which overlooked the Plaza. Sure enough, a sign announced The End of the Universe Café. Sal was sitting at a table by the window. Beside her was a look-alike, same plaid skirt, same navy twin-set. Were they visiting from some school? It was difficult to tell their age, but they seemed older than schoolgirls. And there was something about their eyes. They were a very dark blue and they glittered.

"This is Peanut," said Sal. "We would like to buy Valmai tea but we do not have the financial resources."

I readily agreed to pay for us all and returned from the counter with the cups on a tray. As I was arranging them in front of each of us, Sal said, "It would be best if Valmai did not look directly at us, but at the vase of flowers instead."

Automatically I fixed my gaze on the glass vase which held a few plastic blooms.

Sal continued, "We are here to study human consciousness and behavior. The trouble with you humans is that you have not learned to control reproduction."

I was beginning to feel slightly odd as I stared at the vase and listened to Sal expand her theory. Peanut simply listened. I sipped my tea in silence.

Then Sal said in her abrupt manner, "We are meeting in the building at the foot of Morada Lane tonight. Perhaps Valmai would like to join us." I said nothing and she added, "But perhaps Valmai is not ready for us."

Instantly, I decided that Valmai was definitely not ready. "Thank you, but I have to go," I said and stood before they could change my mind. Later, when I told Susanna about Sal and Peanut, she cautioned me. "I know that building at the foot of Morada Lane. I've never seen anyone there and I've never seen anyone in town who fits your description. If I were you I'd stay away from those people."

When I told my husband, David, about my tea with Sal and Peanut, there was silence at the other end of the phone. Then he said, "You know, I've never really believed in extraterrestrials, but these two sound like the real thing. They came here, picked up a packet of salted peanuts and saw a picture of schoolgirls in uniform. What a pity you didn't take notes!"

I never saw Sal and Peanut again and I was relieved. Those glittering dark blue eyes had made me uneasy. Later, I heard about the petroglyph rock which bordered Pueblo land up at Mabel's. "It's ancient," a woman at Caffé Tazza told me. "They say that extraterrestrials use it as a landing marker."

The Taos Hum

"What's that humming noise?" My friend Meredith and her young daughter, Tegan, had finally come to visit. We'd been for dinner at The Apple Tree on Bent Street, and had just pulled into my parking area.

"What hum? I don't hear anything."

"That low, deep humming."

"Maybe it's the gas meter."

Meredith looked at me with some irritation. "It's not a gas meter. It's a low humming sound." We sat there in the car for a few moments, then she said. "You know what it reminds me of? When I was growing up, there was a Marconi plant right near the border of Montreal and Town of Mount Royal. It made a sound like this."

Throughout the week Meredith continued to hear the humming. I heard nothing and forgot about it. Then one morning at Caffé Tazza, several weeks after my guests had departed, I overheard a conversation at the next table.

"I had another bad night," a woman told her friend. "It's that damned hum again. It stopped for a while, now it's back. It's deep down and scary."

"Yeah," her friend was sympathetic. "They say there are tunnels under Taos that go way down deep into the earth and extraterrestrials use them for experiments."

"Well maybe they could be a bit quieter with those experiments whatever they may be."

Later I would repeatedly hear similar conversations. I decided to do a touch of research. The low deep hum Meredith complained of was reported in Bristol, England in the 1950s, then later in the 1970s around Bondi Beach, Australia. Later still in Windsor, Ontario, Canada and in the 1990s in Taos. Apparently only two percent of people have the hearing range to pick up this deep end of the spectrum. Opinions on what might be the source of the hum vary; low wave electronic frequencies, movements within the earth. To this day, The Taos Hum remains one of those mysteries open to folkloric embellishments like the conversations which enlivened my mornings at Caffé Tazza.

Homage to Mabel: The Salon

"Please come down here soon," Mabel wrote to Gertrude Stein from the Villa Curonia in Florence. "The house is full of pianists, painters, pederasts, prostitutes and peasants. Great material."

Pianist Arthur Rubinstein wrote of his meeting there, "Mabel Dodge was a young woman of around thirty with a pleasant face, a slightly too generous figure, and a fixed, absent smile of a Mona Lisa. She spoke in monosyllables, save when addressing her servants, and she answered any query with a short nod. Life at her Villa Curonia was a constant carousel. Our hostess showed a gift for gathering together the most incongruous combination of guests in the world. There was the art and music critic Carl Van Vechten, a genius at arguing; Robin de la Condamine, a charming, stuttering actor whom nobody had seen on a stage; John Reed, a journalist and poet, and a militant Communist, was sullen and very aggressive. He was Mabel's choice companion. There were two shrieking Englishwoman. We had Gertrude Stein, engaged in some interminable vocal battles with Van Vechten, Reed hating everything and everybody, Norman Douglas, using with relish his most profane repertoire in swearing, and last, but not least, myself, persistently jealous and irritable. Whenever or whatever I played, whether Beethoven or Stravinsky, some of those present would leave the room, hating the one or the other."[50]

When Mabel returned to New York she noted that there seemed to be so many people with important things to say, but no central place in which to meet and discuss the new ideas. Once she finished decorating 23 Fifth Avenue, that white place so ready for new beginnings, she opened her Wednesday salons to the new movement.

"Imagine a stream of human beings passing in and out.. Socialists, Trade Unionists, Anarchists, Suffragists, Poets, Lawyers, Murderers, "Old Friends," Psychoanalysts, IWWs. Single Taxers, Birth Controlists, Newspapermen, Artists, Modern Artists, Clubwomen, Woman's-place-is-in-the-home Women, Clergymen and just plain men there, and stammering in an unaccustomed freedom a kind of speech called Free, exchanged a variousness in vocabulary called, in euphemistic optimism, Opinions!"[51]

By now my life was thoroughly steeped in Mabel's world. On sunny days I could see the "Lawrence women" lounging beneath wide-brimmed hats in the courtyard or in the shade of the portals. I pictured O'Keeffe, dressed in black, her hair pulled back, heading into the Pueblo sage with her easel, hear the sounds of laughter as glasses clinked and the sun sank behind the Sangre de Christos. I imagined possible topics of conversation.

"I've been thinking," I said to Susanna as we took the sun one February lunch time out behind the bookstore. The light was so bright we needed our sunglasses. "Wouldn't it be fun to have a salon?"

Susanna thought. "Yes, it would," she said with her endearing enthusiasm.

We decided to use my little house because it was an easy walk from town. Because my sitting room could only hold five people comfortably on the L-shaped sofa, we decided once a month, to invite three people; we didn't know the wide swarth of characters Mabel attracted, so we settled for poets, writers and painters. We could read, discuss our work and exchange ideas.

While it was doubtful that our modest salon at 220 Morada Lane would have any redeeming social importance, people showed up and took it seriously. We discussed why we were in Taos and what we hoped to achieve in our work. We all had fun and looked forward to our homegrown Wednesday evenings.

Years later, Susanna and I reminisced.

"Remember the garlic bread we served?" I began.

"Of course. And the spaghetti," said Susanna. "And don't forget the cheap red wine."

"But I don't remember anything I read. I was writing my book about a group of people with terminal diseases, but I can't remember reading from it. Do you remember what you read?"

"I do. Because I'm a painter, I had to think carefully about what I wanted to present. I decided to read a piece I'd prepared once at school about Hornbaek, the little fishing village on the coast of Denmark where my mother used to take us for the summers to run free. "

"Yes, I remember," I told her. "When you arrived, your older sister would take your little red shoes to the shoemaker and have metal protectors put on. As you were reading, I could smell the ocean and see the sand dunes. You could pick gooseberries and your mother made wild rosehip soup with a dollop of cream. Yummy. "

"Actually," said Susanna. "What I remember most about our Taos salons was how kind and friendly and supportive we all were of each other. It felt so good."

Mabel had inspired us to launch those little salons, to share our work with a confidence we might not have felt elsewhere. With her restless mind and undaunted spirit, though she'd received criticism of every kind, nobody had accused her of not being authentic. As I read more of her work, I admired her willingness to be self-critical, to keep close to the bone.

At the end of the twentieth century, few young women managed to escape the dull and predictable and remain authentic. Mabel had the means to do as she chose, where and with whom, and she did. She was one of the early rebels and paved the way for a whole new generation of free-thinkers heading west.

By the time of her death in 1962, the war in Vietnam would contribute to another wave of rebels. The hippies who left the big cities and flocked to the New Buffalo commune northwest of town were also seeking new beginnings.

After Dennis Hopper bought Mabel's, it continued to attract artistic rebels through the late sixties and into the seventies. The cultural centers which developed at Mabel's over the next decades, continued Mabel's tradition and focused on personal growth through authentic expression.

Mabel's Pooch: Rescuing Aslan

It was clear from Mabel's writing and from what Phoebe Cottam had told me that dogs had played an important role in Mabel's life. Dogs from the pack who chased Phoebe's little Sealyham terrier up the stairs of the Two-Story House, to Tito, the little red fox-like stray who wandered in and stayed, to her two great Danes, Thyla and Donska.

My favorite story was the coming of Pooch. One summer, Mabel had been out driving when a small black dog came tearing along down the middle of the road towards her. She stopped the car and the little dog "sprang over the closed door and into the seat beside me, a little black bulldog as thin as a shad, with two bat ears sticking up, and wild laughter on its face. She was old and haggard, toothless and worn. Her backbone stuck out through her shabby black coat, so one could count every knob on it."[52]

A girl and her husband came out from a house and told Mabel the dog was eleven or twelve. She slept in the garage at night. "Isn't that too cold?" asked Mabel.

"Yes, I guess so," the man answered. Clearly the little dog had taken matters into her own hands.

I loved Mabel's observation that, "In her eagerness and tenacity for living, she suddenly appeared to resemble my Grandma Ganson so strongly that the curious idea occurred to me that she was my grandma in another shape."[53]

Mabel paid the couple five dollars and a triumphant Pooch took up residence at the Big House. As she drove off beside Mabel, Pooch looked "perfectly at home and full of confidence. The anguished look had faded out of her face and a pleasant smile illumined it."

Mabel's relationship with Pooch strengthened my feelings of connection with Mabel, for without Bianca, I simply would not have come to Taos.

Seven years earlier I had never even heard of a borzoi. Then one morning as I was driving to McGill, just a few blocks before I turned off to Hosmer House, where I taught, a man appeared on the sidewalk with the most extraordinary dog. It was tall and lean with a long silky white coat, and it seemed to prance and float. I pulled abruptly into the curb, to a loud honking from the car behind me.

I jumped out of the car and rushed up to the man. "What sort of dog is that?" I asked him. He stared at the madwoman who had just provoked the morning traffic.

"It's a borzoi," he said politely. "A Russian wolfhound."

The borzoi gazed at me with liquid dark eyes in an elongated face.

"I have to have one," I told him. By now I had created a traffic hazard, so I leapt back into the car. The seed had been planted.

Mabel believed in daily miracles. I too believe in magic. I have to, because time and time again, it has directed my life. Chance meetings, bizarre timings like the realtor's driving me to 220 Morada Lane. This time the magic moved in a similar way, for two days later a friend called to invite me to a dog show.

I'd rarely attended a dog show. If I thought of them at all I'd envision a bunch of tediously groomed animals forced to parade in a most unnatural way, in much the same way I thought of a beauty pageant. This time however, I pricked up my ears and agreed enthusiastically, and that is how, Saturday morning, my friend and I walked into the judging ring as the borzoi entered. And I saw her. She looked straight at me with laughing, rebellious dark eyes that said, I'm not really taking this seriously. She was a silvery white with just the a few shadows of what the breed calls "champagne." Her long silky coat rippled as she pranced around the ring with the other six young lovelies.

"Stack your bitches," ordered the tweed-clad British judge. The handlers brought their dogs to a halt and positioned them; back legs one slightly ahead of the other, long, long nose straight ahead. Motionless.

The judge moved along the line. When she came to my dog, she ran her hands over every inch, opened her mouth and checked her teeth. The borzoi and I locked eyes and I swear she said, "Isn't this ridiculous?" Finally the judge pulled my girl out with two other dogs and the small crowd cheered and clapped as she was awarded the blue ribbon.

I knew we belonged together but I had to convince her owner. As it turned out, luck once more was on my side. The woman, a dentist, owned four borzoi. She was engaged to another dentist, from Boston. She planned to move down there after the marriage but her fiancée did not appear to be overly enthusiastic about having four enormous borzoi sharing their space. She agreed to sell me the dog, whose name, it turned out was Almaza, Russian for "white diamond."

"I'll sell her to you but you won't be able to take her until tomorrow night," the owner told me. "She's won best of bitches in her class, and now she'll compete with the dogs." By dogs, I learned she meant the males of the species. I agreed, but insisted she take my check right away.

It was a good thing I did, for Sunday, my girl won not just Best of Breed (BOB) but Best In Show (BIS) against the winners of all other breeds. Now her owner was less enthusiastic about the sale. I was, however, adamant.

"Do you know how much she's worth now?" her former owner asked me.

I didn't, nor did I care. Almaza leapt into the back seat of my car, which she filled completely, and together we sparkled out of the parking lot, triumphant.

David was in Vermont at the rambling old house, built in 1840, that we were spending every weekend restoring. I drove up with my borzoi, reached in and took her leash and we made our triumphant entrance. Of course David and Bianca adored each other. The moment I clipped off the leash, she took off, running through the house like the wild thing she was.

She started in the living room where she jumped on the sofa, dug in her paws and flipped the sofa cushions on the floor. Then she headed up the front staircase into the bedrooms where she leapt on each bed and tossed the pillows on the floor. We followed, mesmerized, as she traveled through the long wing of bedrooms wreaking havoc. Then she ran lightly down the back stairs, paused in the living room and defecated on the Persian rug we'd inherited from David's parents.

"I told you I was untamed," she said, her dark eyes sparkling defiantly. We put her out on the overgrown tennis court where we had not yet put up the net, carefully latching the gate. "You can have a good run here," I told her. The moment we took our eyes off her she managed to unlatch the gate, cross the lawn and take off down the middle of our country road. When we leapt in the car to follow her she was racing away at over thirty miles an hour. Fortunately she was not quite a year old and lacked the stamina to go far. We retrieved her, flopped in the roadside ditch in a patch of mud.

Somehow Almaza became Bianca and it was clear the dog had never been house-trained but had lived outdoors, kenneled with her mother, sister and brother. We entered a period of intensive training. I simply tied her leash to my wrist. Wherever I went, she went, including McGill, where my students were thoroughly charmed. A borzoi at classes in elegant Hosmer House with its beautifully carved ceilings and refined fixtures, seemed to me an appropriate setting for this quirky dog of the doomed czars. In actual fact, her presence was so out of the expected that nobody even thought to question. She'd lie quietly beside me while I taught and afterwards I'd take her for long, long walks on Mount Royal, the mountain park in the center of the city.

One evening I finished work late, and by the time we crossed the road up from Hosmer House to the mountain, it was almost dark, with a fine mist descending. As usual, Bianca was at the end of the wind-out leash. Then out from behind the trees a man approached us. Something about him felt not right. Quick as a flash, Bianca leapt towards him, baring her perfect long white teeth. The man took off.

From that moment on I knew my dog would always protect me. Some time after, I was working at home in my office with its view of the small back courtyard and next-door woodland. A man was working in front of the house, repairing the old stone wall.

"If you need to come into the back to do the wall, just let me know. My dog can be dangerous," I warned him. He looked at the long-haired beauty beside me and I could tell he didn't believe a word I said.

By this point, Bianca's training had progressed rapidly and she could roam freely through the house and courtyard. Suddenly a pair of jean-clad legs came dangling over the wall to the courtyard. This was followed by a flash of white and the cloth seat of his pants was neatly removed. In a flash, both legs vanished back over the wall and Bianca returned to sunning herself. Neither the workman nor I ever mentioned the incident.

By the end of the month Bianca was perfectly house-trained. I could and did, take her everywhere and she would always come when called. Borzoi are sight hounds and predictably unreliable. If they feel like coming when you call them they'll oblige. If there's anything more interesting, however, like a squirrel, they remain deaf to your call. Not Bianca.

I'd take her several times a day to a park close to McGill, a park with a high brick wall around it which had been bequeathed to the dogs of the city by a delightful man called Percy Walters. You had to be careful though, because sometimes the tall wrought iron gates were left open. I started by attaching a very long cord to Bianca's collar then letting her go as far afield as it would allow. Then I'd call, "Bianca come" and pull lightly on the cord. I'd praise her to the hilt and never needed a food treat. When she came one hundred per cent of the time, I decided to check the gates, then let her free. She took off, running stretched flat-out, her plumy tail a silver apostrophe. Round and round the perimeter of the park she flew, a glorious sun-filled unicorn.

Then came the moment I'd been working towards now for over a month.

"Bianca come," I called. She came to a halt. Then without so much as a second thought, she raced toward me and stopped, her long tongue dripping, dark eyes filled with fun.

One afternoon just before Christmas, my daughter, Tilke, and I were in Santa Fe doing our holiday shopping. Bianca was with us as we browsed in the little UNICEF store down one of the narrow streets off the plaza. A woman approached. "Is that one of the dogs they rescued?" she asked.

Tilke and I looked blank. Then I said, "No, I've had her since she was a year old and now she's eight. I don't know about the rescue dogs."

She told me the sad story. The Santa Fe Animal Shelter had been called out to rescue forty-two borzoi. Their breeder had left California after she had been charged for puppy-milling borzoi in her basement. That hadn't stopped her. She'd simply taken the dogs, left the state and set up shop once more a few miles outside Albuquerque in the desert, where in a fenced field, the dogs had managed to survive any way they could, the breeder visiting them once a week with food and water. Some were found dead. Others had managed to survive by eating birds. All were skin and bones by the time the Shelter rescued them and brought them into its headquarters on Cerrillos Road. That was back before a wonderful new facility was donated on the outskirts of town.

We picked up David from where he was selecting his Christmas presents from Collected Works bookstore, and the three of us discussed visiting the Shelter. We agreed it was the right thing to do. "It all depends on Bianca," I said. "If she's happy with another borzoi I'll do it."

We drove out on Cerrillos Road, the Santa Fe commercial strip. As we approached the Shelter, we heard the howls of the homeless. As it turned out, it was not the borzoi howling. People had rallied to foster them, driving from all over New Mexico as well as Colorado and Texas. By now, the only borzoi that remained were those with some physical defect, and a few older dogs. They stood, perfectly quiet and watched us as we approached. I was drawn to the male dog in a corner pen.

The dog looked at me through his one good eye. The other was clouded and bluish. A healthy borzoi is slender. Tilke once observed, "Bianca is two-dimensional." This big borzoi, inches taller than Bianca, was dry, lusterless white and red fur around flesh stretched thin across bones that looked as though they might snap at any moment. His teeth were rotten, his breath smelled terrible.

We looked at each other. "Could I take him out to the parking lot and see if he'll walk with my borzoi?" I asked the attendant. She nodded and opened the gate. We scarcely needed a leash, the dog could barely hobble. In the end we brought Bianca to him. She stood and looked at him. He was almost too weak to raise his head. Then she walked over to him and pressed her nose against his side. As we watched, the dog raised his head. A small movement. Then his tail moved to the side.

We lifted the big, shockingly light borzoi onto Bianca's padded bed in the trunk of the Explorer. Bianca jumped onto the back seat beside Tilke. We offered him water but he lay motionless. We drove slowly up through that twisting road through the Rio Grande. A light snow was starting to fall as we pulled into Morada Lane.

We carried the big boy in and placed him on the snow-covered grass. He was too weak to lift his leg, but simply squatted. His urine made a patch of dark yellow on the fresh snow. He refused the cooked turkey hamburger we offered and fell asleep on Bianca's big, soft, dog bed, which we brought in from the car.

Next morning when I woke, Bianca was not in the room. The living room was sunny and we found her lying quietly beside the new dog. When we opened the door for her into the garden, this time the big boy managed to limp along behind her.

Bianca healed that dog. She never left his side. At feeding time she lay beside him until he'd finished eating. I still have a black and white photo of them, lying on the snow, each with a dish of food between their front paws.

It took two weeks before he was strong enough to walk the few houses up the lane to Mabel's. We found him a gentle, sweet fellow but it was clear he'd been not only neglected but brutalized. When he finally became strong enough for surgery, I took him in to see Bianca's vet and have some tooth extractions and a deep cleaning. The vet called me. "Your dog just bit me," he said. When I went in, the vet's hand was wrapped in a bandage. The bite had required stitches, but the vet never did seem to hold a grudge. He saw too many mistreated dogs.

Later, the dog, whom we christened Aslan, bit David as well. Not a serious bite, just a skin graze but it was worrying. We couldn't just let our dog go around biting people.

One morning I startled him when I opened the door to the

greenhouse too quickly. He lunged at me and I heard myself shout. "No, Aslan." The big red and white dog stopped and looked at me. Then he dropped his head, sidled up beside me, found my hand. I felt his warm tongue lick my wrist. I knew then, he would never bite again. He never did.

One morning I received a phone call from the Santa Fe Animal Shelter. They were bringing a court case against the breeder. Technically, as they had informed me at Christmas, my dog was "seized property" and did not belong to me until the outcome of the court case was decided.

"What are the chances of your winning the case?" I asked the director who was calling me. There was a moment of silence, then she said slowly. "New Mexico is not known for its attention to animals. You know it doesn't always treat its children the way it should. We'll need all the help we can get."

Fortunately, my friend, Meredith Webster, was on the board of The American Humane Society. Her work involved things like making sure that animals used in movie productions were humanely treated. When I explained Aslan's situation to her she, I knew she would come up with the best plan.

"We have to talk to the DA," she told me. "Inspire him. Give me his number and I'll call him." She did. He was a young guy without experience in animal-cruelty cases. Meredith had colleagues from the AHA phone and guide him. By the time the case was called up, he was both fully informed and inspired.

I drove down to Santa Fe for the case. This time however, I decided to leave Bianca and Aslan in Taos. Better, I reasoned, not to have Aslan at hand, just in case the DA lost and the breeder was awarded her dogs. I would leave the dogs in the house and Susan-next-door offered to let them into the garden and feed them.

The trial was at the old grey stone courthouse just off Washington. I was heartened to meet many of the people who were fostering the dogs, together with a small crowd of animal activists. A full hand of reporters were there. We stood around outside for an hour. To the north, great black clouds began to roll in.

Finally a man came out. "The case has been canceled for today," he told us. "We'll let you know the rescheduling." No explanation. I went up to one of the people from the Animal Shelter. "What happens if the case doesn't come up for months?" I asked. "I'm due back in Montreal soon."

He looked me straight in the eyes. "Valmai, I can't tell you what to do, but sometimes our dogs just disappear." I blinked back tears. "Thank you," I said.

By now, the storm was brewing, the whole sky had turned black and a vicious wind ripped at my coat as I dashed for the car. As I drove back up to Taos, the howling gale was gathering force. By the time I reached Espanola it broke, and the windshield turned white with hailstones the size of robins' eggs.

When I finally reached Taos, eager to get back to my borzoi, I replayed those words, "sometimes our dogs just disappear." I stopped at the local burger joint and bought Bianca and Aslan each a juicy half-pounder.

Next morning all was calm. I drove the borzoi out in the canyon and we walked for almost an hour, climbing into the hills to where we could look down on the town. Bianca of course, always came when I called and Aslan was her shadow.

By this time he had gained weight and his coat was beginning to grow glossy.

Once, as we climbed, Bianca disappeared. When I called she did not appear and there was no sign of Aslan, either. I called again. Nothing. Then as I climbed higher, suddenly Bianca leapt out at me from behind a tree, laughing. Aslan, his tail wagging vigorously was right behind. As we descended, I felt a great wave of happiness with my companions.

When the case finally was called up, I was back in Montreal with my dogs. One of the reporters who'd covered the case filled me in on the details.

"You're not going to believe this," he began. "I've never known anything like it. It's a first for New Mexico! They got the breeder on every single count. Turns out she's a Russian woman who started with a good Russian bloodline and used to be a legitimate breeder. Then something happened, who knows? She went bad and started hoarding and puppy-milling. Well, they sentenced her to prison, guilty on every count, let me repeat, and on the way from the court room, she took a bottle of pills out of her purse and swallowed them, so she ended up in hospital having her stomach pumped out. It was quite a day. Oh, and the DA was a real hero!"

By the time of the court case every one of the forty two borzoi had found a home, people driving from as far away as Illinois. The last dog, an elderly lady the people at the Shelter called Granny, had a mouthful of rotting teeth. We were so grateful for the gift of Aslan, we arranged to have her teeth, like Aslan's, taken care of. Shortly after, Granny was also adopted.

The Darker Side

I first noticed the droppings as I cleaned behind the toaster, about half a dozen, unmistakably mouse. Under the coffee maker and the blender as well. I disliked finding mouse droppings for several reasons. The most obvious was basic hygiene. Mice carry disease, especially in New Mexico where some years ago, everyone panicked when a healthy young man, a cross-country runner, in fact, dropped dead en route to his wife's funeral. She had died of severe respiratory distress. His lungs appeared to have filled with fluid, causing what amounted to drowning. I'm not sure how, but they managed to identify the cause of death, his and hers, as a potentially lethal respiratory bug first identified in South Korea as the Hanta virus.

I considered the irony of my situation. Woman goes to Taos to escape bronchitis and dies of mouse-dropping virus contracted from cleaning behind the toaster. How long, I wondered, would it be before someone discovered my decomposing body? Would Bianca and Aslan, crazed with hunger, begin to gnaw on my remains the way Manby's guard dogs had attacked his severed head?

I bought a face mask and heavy-duty rubber gloves, the one's with a thick lining, and cleaned as carefully as I could with bleach. Clearly the dogs did not approve of the smell. They wrinkled their long borzoi noses and whined to go out.

When it appeared I was not on the threshold of drowning in my own fluids, I cautiously inspected the area behind the toaster. Sure enough there was a small pile of fresh droppings. This time I drove into town to buy a packet of Decon. I didn't feel good about the choice and at Randall's Lumber something prevented me from administering an agonizing poison to my rodent visitors.

I looked at a selection of wooden mouse-traps but the thought of coming out in the morning to the crumpled corpse of a mouse stirred memories and guilt that I thought had long been forgotten.

I trained myself not to jump when a mouse darted across the kitchen floor, scurried from behind the toaster and across the kitchen window sill. I lost my appetite for cinnamon toast. The problem wasn't its mousehood, nor was I actually fearful of catching the Hanta virus. It went much deeper.

When I was nine years old I became what the books referred to as a "mouse-fancier." It all began when a school friend invited me to meet Roger.

"You'll love Roger," she'd told me.

Roger turned out to be a carpet snake who hung out in the heated linen closet.

"What does he eat?" I asked as we viewed the plump coils on the shelf below the fluffy bath towels.

"Mice. He eats them whole. Want to watch?"

I didn't, but somehow I watched the entire awful process, mesmerized by this horrible monster in the linen closet.

I left her house with Roger's rescued breakfast snuggled in the pocket of my jacket. I named that white mouse Felix and carried him wherever I went, tucked down my shirt. I don't recall his droppings and small wet puddles bothering me at all.

A month or so later I became ambitious for more. Wouldn't it be fun to have different colored mice? Once again, I raided Roger's pantry. Along came Rosinante, a sleek black female, or in mouse-fanciers' lingo, a doe. Then I added Taffy, a honey-colored doe.

Mice breed, like mice. Six months later I had seventy five of the charming little rodents. My big brother Arthur, who loved any scientific challenge, built me an elaborate mouse mansion. Made from a plywood packing crate that had once housed our gas stove, he stood it on its side and covered the front with the fine mesh screening that back then, we referred to as "fly wire."

Pleased with his work, he built a series of wooden nesting boxes which he hammered to the outside, high up at the back. His design encouraged the mice to reach their bedrooms via a cunning selection of ladders and holes.

It seemed that every time I opened the tops of the bedrooms and gazed down into the cotton balls that I changed once a week, there was a new litter of hairless pink babies, their bulging eyelids still fused, squeaking up a storm.

I did my best to name each mouse. This period of my life coincided with my becoming not just a mouse fancier but also a balletomane; my favorite white doe became Odette and her black sister, Odile. My stud, second only to Felix, was a handsome long-tailed fellow called Prince Siegfried. Their reproductive activities quickly filled the pages of a fat black book labeled in gold, stick-on letters, "Breeding Records." Cleverly, my brother had designed the cage to isolate pairs of breeding mice by a series of wooden partitions.

Felix turned out to be a prodigious stud who appeared to cast his favors equally among the members of his harem. He grew fat and prosperous, the biggest white mouse I'd ever seen. No longer did he run up and down the ladders or pedal away inside the revolving wheel. In fact, by day, he didn't appear to do much of anything.

The moment the sun went down he sprang into action. I wasn't sure whether it was his surging testosterone or the bread and milk of which he was exceedingly fond. Then one day he escaped. I found him in the garden not far from Mouse Mansion. He was resting dreamily in the shade of my blue soap bush, the one where if you took water and rubbed some of the flowers between your palms, you could make a splendid lather.

He seemed so happy that after this, I allowed Felix the free run of the garden. We were between cats and my dog, Chips, was a tolerant fellow.

It wasn't until I caught glimpses of two small white mice behind the roses that I became uneasy. Felix had lovely pink eyes. These little mice had dark eyes and their fur wasn't quite the snowy white of their father's. Then one morning I saw the mother. She was unmistakably brown. A wild brown mouse, to be precise, breeding up a dynasty with old Felix. I tried to catch their offspring but they were quick as the wild.

I examined my meticulous breeding records. Rosinante, my first black doe, had bred with Felix and I now had three boxes of beige mice, six coveted palominos and even a spotted mouse.

Taffy, my honey-colored doe, had bred with both Felix and Prince Siegfried. They'd produced five pages of multi-colored offspring. The pages of my book were almost filled. So was Mouse Mansion. "I need another cage," I told my brother, but he was of a practical nature and declined. "You've got too many mice. Get rid of some."

I set off on my bike, the black one I pretended was a stallion called Flyaway, up the steep hill to the S. and G. Pet Shop. Nobody seemed to know what S. and G. stood for, so I dubbed it Sludge and Grimble. The shop reeked of chlorine, I recognized it because it reminded me of the Public Swimming Baths. Did they clean the fish tanks with it, or perhaps use it to drown out the mouse smells? Mice have a distinctive odor, strong and sickly sweet and my corner of the garden, hidden behind tall, well clipped privet hedges, was beginning to smell, particularly as we plunged into the hot sticky Melbourne summer.

The man at Sludge and Grimble agreed to buy half a dozen of my mice for a penny a mouse. I pedaled home, licking the ice cream cone my enterprise had yielded.

As the summer unfolded and the grass turned dry and dusty, I tried to separate the males from the females, first making sure I identified each correctly by holding it up by the tail as my mouse book recommended. But if it's a young mouse, the gender isn't always easy to diagnose, especially when it's dangling upside down. In the following month it became clear that there was a substantial margin of error.

When Mother complained of a white mouse in her snapdragons , I knew the game was up. That day after school, I loaded a dozen mice into a cardboard grocery box and cycled up the hill to Sludge and Grimble.

"We'll buy this lot, but these'll keep us going for a while," said the man I'd labeled Mr. Sludge. Triumphant, I squandered my earnings at the fish and chip shop next door which smelled of vinegar and the greasy newspaper used to parcel up the goodies.

The beginning of the end occurred when I stepped plunk in the middle of a mouse nest. It was buried just under a patch of fragrant pink clover by the soap bush. The beige mother scuttled out from under my feet, squeaking. When I parted the grass, my stomach churned. I'd squashed a batch of hairless pink babies.

Suddenly all the mice, hitherto charming, seemed somehow menacing and maggoty. That afternoon I did my best to catch the garden mice with a plate of bread and milk. Six gave themselves up. I loaded them, together with six of my white mice, into the grocery box and once more pedaled up the hill. This time Mr. Sludge was not pleased to see me.

"We don't need any more mice," he said. "What am I supposed to do with them?"

"You could have a sale," I told him. He didn't seem at all keen. Finally I persuaded him to take them, for free.

I donated another box to Roger the carpet snake. Then on my evening inspection of the nest boxes I surprised Rosinante, my oldest doe. She was crouched over her nest of cotton wool. Around her was bloody carnage. Heads, tiny pink body parts. My mouse had become a cannibal.

I rounded up every mouse I could find and stuffed them in a pillowcase. Then I tied a rock to the corner. The tin wash troughs in the laundry house were deep. I ran water until the trough was full. Then I tried not to notice the struggles as I lowered the pillowcase into the deep water.

Two months later, when Felix, my only surviving mouse, developed a large tumor on his side, I drowned him too. But the mouse problem was far from over. It was rare that either of my parents went as far down in the garden as my hedged-in hideaway. They preferred the lawns and gardens and the shady patios beneath pergolas dripping with passion fruit and honeysuckle. As long as I appeared at mealtimes with freshly-washed hands and participated intelligently in the conversation, I was free to spend my time as I chose.

I think my parents had some vague idea of a pet white mouse, but I hadn't dared tell them about the grotesque outcome of my genetic experiments. Mother would inevitably say, "Well dear, you'll have to think it out for yourself." My father would possibly be angry at my lack of responsibility.

Months after I drowned the mice, my very proper English mother, weeding her rose garden, unearthed a litter of those hideous hairless pink mouse pups. She screamed. The following week we acquired a pair of grey and white cats. I tried not to look as they chewed the tiny bones in front of me.

I felt condemned. Deep down and forever, I would carry with me my terrible secret. I was a murderer. I never wanted to see another mouse.

Now, thirty years later, the Mouse of Taos continued to scurry along my counters in the dead of night. At Christmas, the tiny house filled with guests and yummy treats. The most obsessive housekeeper would have had a time of it keeping the counter crumb-free.

Christmas Eve, Tilke, refusing to abandon her childhood tradition with Santa Claus, set out a plate of gingerbread cookies for the Merry Old Man. I'd meant to eat them myself before bed but we walked out to admire the stars and when we returned I simply forgot. The Mouse had a little party of its own. Next morning Tilke announced, "Look Santa must have liked his cookies."

By New Year the rodent had become almost insolent, lingering a moment before it slouched down behind the sink. One evening as I was reading in front of the fireplace, it ventured further than its usual territory, across the kitchen floor and towards me in the sitting room. I stomped my feet. "Shoo! Scat." Aslan and Bianca cocked their ears but didn't bother to move. So far they'd shown not the slightest interest in hunting. Though bred to hunt wolves, attached to long coursing leashes held by horsemen, then chase and hold down the wolf, clearly they considered a mouse unworthy of their attention.

Then one afternoon, the mouse sprang out at me from behind my favorite blue and white teacup. I squealed. My heart was pounding and I began to brood on the fate of this tenacious little rodent. I lay on the couch and gazed into the fire while outside wind sighed and snow fell in large flakes.

Suddenly a scene surfaced from a forgotten corner of my childhood. I kept the floor of Mouse Mansion carpeted with a thick layer of sawdust. A twenty minute bike ride from my house, on the other side of the river, was a small sawmill. If I waited 'til the afternoon whistle blew and the men left for the day, I could sneak in and fill my cardboard box, which fit snugly in the basket of my bike. Each load lasted about two weeks.

One day after school, I'd just filled my box and was carrying it through the deserted mill yard when a man appeared in front of me. He was big, with red hands and a lumpy face. He smiled but didn't say a word. His teeth looked as though he'd forgotten to brush.

I stood clutching my box of sawdust. Was I going to get into trouble for stealing? I was about to tell him about my mice when he squatted down in front of me. Then he reached under my plaid skirt and cupped the crotch of my white cotton underpants. I froze. Why was he doing that? From the time I was four, my parents had instructed me never to get into a car with a stranger, nor to accept sweets. "What will you do if someone offers you a sweet?" They drilled me. The correct answer was, "I shall throw them in the gutter." But for some reason, though my mother has since assured me that my pronunciation was normally clear and precise at age four, my response came out, "I shall throw them in the duttah." Which made my brother snicker.

The man in the mill yard wasn't offering any sweets, nor was there any sign of a car to lure me into, but I felt scared. I dropped my box and the cloud of sawdust made the man cough. I bolted as fast as I could towards my bike, leapt on and pedaled across the little bridge and up the hills, not stopping 'til I reached the quiet houses and thick gardens overhung by old shade trees. I never returned.

That night as I lay in bed in my little house on Morada Lane, I knew for certain that it was time for The Mouse of Taos to move on. Next morning I arrived at Randall's Lumber a few moments after the store opened. My favorite salesman greeted me. He had kind brown eyes and long yellow teeth. He'd helped me unblock my sink, measured and cut glass for a broken window and instructed me in the art of removing the molding to install and putty in the new glass.

"I want a mousetrap," I told him. "not the kind that kills, one where you catch and release."

"I get it, you don't want to kill the mouse." He grinned conspiratorily, "Well, let's see what we can find."

He left the cash unattended and I followed him down the creaking wooden aisle past cans of roofing paint and weather stripping.

"This is what we want." He was pointing at a whole arsenal of mouse-fighting equipment; conventional mousetraps, Decon and several other poisons. On the bottom shelf was a pile of yellow boxes. Painted on the top lid was a sort of cat-in-armor. The cat wore a red waistcoat, Superman style, decorated with a yellow mouse. Victor Tin Cat, it said in a flourish. Repeating Mouse Trap. *Trampa Repetidora Para Ratones*.

I read the list of benefits Victor Tin Cat promised: simple to use; no winding or resetting; holds thirty mice; no bait required; reliable mechanism; quick and easy to service.

"This look like what you want?" My obliging salesman picked up the yellow box. Let's take it up front and have a look. He lifted the Tin Cat from its package. It was a low metal box with a hole at each end and a series of air vents.

"There's another model here too, tell you what, let's take them both up to the desk and check 'em out." He picked up the Tin Cat and another box from the pile next to it.

Back at the desk, he placed Victor on the counter, picked up his pencil and inserted it through one of the holes.

"Here, you try. The mouse comes in here and pushes down here." I inserted my finger and pushed down. Nothing happened.

"Seems a bit stiff. Do you think a mouse is heavy enough to move this?" Leery of gadgets, I was dubious.

"Maybe this other one'll work better." He opened he second box. On the side was a wind-up key. We peered inside.

"It's like this," he said. "The mouse comes in here and this spring catches him and throws him into the box."

"Isn't that cruel?"

"Well," he grinned. "He may have a bit of a concussion. Might have to take him to the vet before you let him go."

"No. I don't want to hurt him."

"Tell you who'd know about the other one. Our manager's real bright, he'd know all about it."

He led me into the nether regions of Randall's, a vast dim expanse where piles of lumber lay stacked beside panes of glass and things like two by four's and quarter rounds. I'd become familiar with them all now in my winters in Taos.

The manager was chatting with two henchmen. He was a handsome man with curly grey hair and a spotless plaid shirt.

"The lady wants one of those mousetraps that don't kill the mouse and she wants to know whether her mouse'll be heavy enough to open the hole."

He produced the Tin Cat and set it on the desk. All three men examined it, pushed their fingers in, passed it among themselves.

"Reckon it'll work," the manager seemed as obliging as my salesman, "but tell you what, if you don't catch your mouse tonight, just bring it back in the morning."

My salesman wrapped the yellow box carefully in brown paper and snipped off the string with a pair of large scissors.

"Keep your receipt." He handed me my copy of the bill, the sort of nice big yellow paper you can't possibly mislay in your purse.

That night before bed, I cut a few wedges of Swiss cheese. Then I opened the Tin Cat and placed them in the middle of the box on the metal bottom. I threw in a few sunflower seeds for good measure. A flurry of scratching and squeaking woke me. The clock said 2:35. Feeling guilty, I tried to fall asleep. Bianca raised her head from near my pillow, Aslan, on his dog bed, didn't stir.

The glowing red numbers on my bedside clock said 4:41 by the time I fell asleep. I'd been thinking of my childhood and the mice and the man at the sawmill.

I woke with the sun and fumbled through the kitchen to let the dogs out. Then I remembered. I had caught The Mouse. Perhaps it was thirsty. So I chopped some celery into tiny thin pieces, ran the cold tap on them and pushed them through the air vents. When I peered in, there was no sign of the creature. The Tin Cat hadn't worked, the mouse had eaten the goodies and escaped.

I was planning to take the trap back after breakfast, when a shadow flicked across the Tin Cat's air vents. This time when I peered in, the mouse was definitely there. It must have hidden beneath the entryway.

I wanted to release it as quickly as possible and finish with mice forever. But where to take it? It didn't seem fair to release it in the wilderness where it would be easy prey for an eagle or coyote. Susan had told me that mice were territorial and would simply return, so I needed to take it far away to make this unlikely. Nor did it seem quite right to release my mouse where it could simply take up residence in someone else's house. Finally, I thought of the ideal place.

I packed a baggie with a mixture of walnuts and almonds and filled a small applesauce container with water. After all, it would be a shock just getting used to a new habitat.

The sun was shining on the snowy cap of the Sacred Mountain and the sky that intense lavender blue. I said goodbye to the dogs and drove out south of town and onto Paseo del Canon. Either side of the road the sage waved in a light wind, an ocean of faded grey-green.

There is a parking place a few minutes along the road where the sage stretches about five hundred yards into a pile of rocks. A short distance beyond is the pleasant adobe building of the Christian Family Church. The mouse is one of God's creatures and if the Almighty didn't want it she could surely do something about it. I had done my bit.

I positioned the nuts and water, then set Victor Tin Cat beside a clump of sage. The earth smelled warm. D. H. Lawrence might have described the smell as fecund. A wispy innocent cloud brushed the blue. Then three things happened simultaneously. I opened the lid of the trap, felt a sharp pain in my finger and the mouse leapt to freedom. When I looked down, my hand was covered with blood. Surely the mouse hadn't bitten me. I was relieved to see that the sharp metal of the lid had cut into the side of my right index finger. There was no sign of The Mouse.

That evening, I imagined every possible disaster. What if she were eaten by an eagle? Or she had a family who were anxiously waiting for her to return with food? I called my friends for reassurance. My newest friend, Angie, who sold delicious macrobiotic meals to support herself and her young son, Hunter, said, "I think it would be a beautiful thing for your mouse to be returned to the earth as eagle droppings."

Susan-next-door said, "Better put the trap out again tonight. Then if the mouse has a family you can release them in the same place. One mouse is cute, a family is disgusting."

I readied the Tin Cat with another sprinkle of sunflower seeds and more wet celery. In the morning a tiny pink nose pressed against the bars, two tiny paws scrabbled at me. I chopped an organic strawberry and pushed it through.

When I released her, for I was now sure that yesterday's mouse had been the male, she jumped to freedom. Then she scampered across the sage towards the Christian Family Church.

That night I slept soundly. In the morning I examined the Tin Cat. This time it was empty. I checked behind the toaster and the coffee maker and the blender. Not a single mouse dropping. I opened the cupboard under the sink and took out my rubber gloves and bottle of bleach. After I finished cleaning every inch of the counter, I made myself a cup of tea and sat in the sun porch to enjoy it. When I realized The Mouse was gone forever I felt a fine sense of relief.

For some time after I released the mouse, I thought about how long I had carried with me my secret and managed to suppress the shame of drowning my pet mice. As I thought about the details of the incident, I realized that my suppression was somehow connected to the man who had groped me in the sawmill. I had never told a soul about either incident, but had walled them off as dirty and disgusting.

Now in my leisurely new life, I finally had an opportunity for reflection and inner discovery. I began to examine old secrets and walled off emotions including my fears about illness. Prior to Taos I'd done my best to simply carry on normally through all those bronchitis winters without taking the time to stop and go deeper.

As I read Mabel's *Intimate Memories*, a particular passage jumped out at me. People accused her of being bored or blasé because she showed no feelings. Mabel wrote that people never suspected the feelings which were building up in her too quickly to attach to anything.

Her words unleashed in me another forgotten memory. At Bennington, my mentor, Nicholas Delbanco, had once accused me of being "pathologically polite." It took a while to figure out how this played out in my writing, but his comment prodded me to explore and acknowledge suppressed emotions as I embarked on my first novel, *The Dreams of Zoo Animals*.

As my new novel *The Loneliness of Angels,* with its cast of seriously ill characters unfolded before me on the page each morning, I finally recognized my own build-up of feelings associated with illness. One particular memory surfaced. I'd joined the Melbourne University Mountaineering Club and after a particularly nasty bout of bronchitis, I was reluctant to admit my hard time keeping up on our weekend hikes. Australians, by and large, tend to value rugged stamina and I wasn't about to be seen as a weakling.

One Easter we set off on what turned out to be a grueling three day hike in rugged terrain. The second afternoon it began to sleet and I had trouble keeping up with the group. When I finally felt dizzy and too weak to continue, I had no choice but to admit defeat. I slunk down the mountain to the nearest small town.

Decades later, sitting there at my old oak table in Taos, I could feel once again the shame of being unable to keep up. As a small child I'd detested being ill, of keeping family awake at night with my incessant coughing. I tried to counteract this by pretending I was vigorously healthy and at school I'd become known for high jump and hurdles.

Looking back, my image of myself as a rugged outdoors person probably stood me in good stead and pushed me to overcome the weakness with which I'd been born. Until my time in Taos my days had been jam-packed with the challenges of career and family. But now, as I continued writing the novel, it was a relief to finally have time to confront all those dark and secretive feelings. Central to my reluctance to view my illness with compassion, was the isolation I'd experienced as a result of ill health.

So many times when I'd felt weak from bronchitis I'd looked at my family and friends around me carrying on vigorously. I'd felt somehow like Hans Christian Andersen's *Little Match Girl*, standing in the cold street at Christmas looking through a window at a happy family celebrating around a festive table.

Mabel's Secret

My journey initiated by the mouse of Morada Lane, led me to suspect that we do our best to block out memories of which we are ashamed. In the following months, as I turned my memories of illness inside out, I wondered whether Mabel concealed, even though in her earliest *Intimate Memories*, she expressed a distaste for keeping secrets. Certainly, her memoirs were frank. She didn't seem to hold back as she described her complex relationships. It wasn't until more than a decade later, when I was no longer living in Taos, but had moved to Santa Fe, that Lois Palken Rudnick's book, *The Suppressed Memoirs of Mabel Dodge Luhan*, was released. In consideration for the family, the manuscripts, held at Yale University's Beinecke Library, were not to be released before the year 2000.

These suppressed memoirs reveal Mabel's struggle with venereal disease. Her sexual relationship with her married gynecologist, while she was still a young mother, gave her gonorrhea. When he confessed that he had a dose of "the clap," Mabel, in her innocence, suggested that she "take it." In a horrifying violation of the young woman, he gave it to her. Gonorrhea is serious, it can cause lasting damage including inflammation and infertility.

It appears that venereal disease was the dark secret of the day. Mabel's second husband, Edwin Dodge, before their marriage confessed that he had syphilis but claimed that he was no longer infectious. Her third husband, Maurice Sterne, had also been infected with syphilis.

The final tragedy came when the man she truly loved, Tony Luhan, also contracted syphilis and infected Mabel.

When she met Tony Lujan, she wrote of the Pueblo dwellers, "They seemed so clean and wholesome and free of the sin and decadence of the world." After she and Tony were married, when he came home one night from the Pueblo, Mabel noticed blood on the white sheet in which the men of the Pueblo wrapped themselves. She smelled semen. He told Mabel he had slept with the wife of his "corn brother." When he then made love to her, Mabel writes, "The smell of seminal fluid was evil and destructive for me." How could it not be? After all, though it was hushed over, her father had died of syphilis and two of her former husbands had carried the ticking bomb of infection.

"Now you have broken everything between us," Mabel told Tony when she found the blood and seminal fluid on his white sheet. "It can never be the same again."

Tony said, "Oh yes. It will always be the same between us. You know it. We are together for always. You know it."

Mabel writes, "Now, I could never get away. I would always have to come back. This thing between us was the unbreakable bondage."

That night, Mabel felt, "a deep, terrible realization of an end of something, the end of our innocent happiness and completion, and the beginning of tragedy."[54]

The morning after, Mabel felt that she had been reborn into a new world, unfamiliar and painful to move in. The following week, she felt a sudden burning when she went to the toilet and discovered a sore swelling. Tony was off on a trip with his friend John Collier.

Mabel drove down to Santa Fe with a visiting friend, where she visited Dr. Mera, the head of Sunmount Sanatorium. She chose to go to Santa Fe, as Doc Martin of Taos, was known to gossip. As they drove down, the burning sensation was so painful that Mabel had to stop and get out of the car several times.

Dr. Mera diagnosed a chancre, the first symptom of syphilis. Mabel records, "The strangest darkness came down on me, shutting out the light."

All her life, throughout her father's struggle with syphilis, then with Edwin Dodge and Maurice Sterne, inevitably, fear of a disease which she had seen kill her father, had stalked her. She told her friend, "I have been scared of it all my life, horrified—and a nightmare to me."

When her friend reassured her that no one need ever know, Mabel said, "I will know."

After that diagnosis she hated her body for the first time. She felt unclean.

When Tony returned from the trip with Collier he had a similar chancre. Both Tony's and Mabel's Wasserman tests were positive.

It wasn't until penicillin became available to the public around 1946 that the horror of syphilis could be cured. Untreated, a person who has contracted syphilis can remain contagious for up to four years. After that, a tertiary phase that can last a lifetime can affect eyesight, hearing, produce skin lesions and also damage the heart. Treatment for syphilis at that time involved shots of an arsenic-based compound called Salvarsan, administered into a vein.

The compound was not without potential side effects including complications to the liver, and while it proved effective in clearing up the initial symptoms, it did not render the person non-contagious. Nor did it prevent the tertiary stage. At first Tony refused to take what Mabel described as a "loathsome cure," though preferable to madness or death, which might result from not taking it. His corn brother died at the pueblo seven years later and the wife, from whom Tony had contracted syphilis, died two years after her husband.

Mabel, a witness to the painful hours that preceded her father's death in his bedroom, had good reason to believe, after three of her four husbands had turned out to be syphilitic, that "the sins of the fathers are visited upon their children." She claimed she had never believed in "secrets" but now she carried the shameful secret of her syphilis. She recalled her irritation helping Sterne deal with the disease and similarly when Dodge had had to go off for water "cure" treatments at Aix Les Bains, for the symptoms can pop up at any time. Syphilis can be passed congenitally and Rudnick speculates in *Suppressed Memories*, about whether Mabel chose to abort Dodge's baby for that reason.

The dark physical cloud syphilis now cast on Mabel's marriage and future health was matched only by her cry that all her life she had been "free as a bird" and now, because of circumstances beyond her control, was forced to give up her liberty.

The extent of syphilitic infection before the 1946 cure by penicillin, was estimated conservatively at around one in ten. Nor was there any support for public education. When Margaret Sanger, a regular at Mabel's New York salon, tried to distribute a pamphlet, *What Every Girl Should Know,*" in 1913, four years before Mabel's arrival in Taos, the U.S. Post Office confiscated it as "obscene," because it actually mentioned gonorrhea and syphilis.

Had the pamphlet be distributed, much misery and many lives could have been saved. Sanger estimated that a staggering number of women in New York were in danger of contracting syphilis upon marriage and if they then became pregnant, a shockingly high number of their babies would die.

Advocating chastity and sexual "purity" was as effective back then as it is today, where the attitude that somehow a woman deserves what she gets from sex, be it a sexually transmitted disease or an unwanted pregnancy, still lingers.

When Mabel, during the period of Salvarsan injections, lost consciousness and remained in a coma for three days, Tony believed she had been dead. In their suffering, they managed to break through the shock of what had happened and though they were never again lovers as they had been, they were never "separate or cold or lost to each other again."[55]

Mabel's doctor, concerned that she had at some time been infected with one of her previous husbands' syphilis, with the coma a possible side effect that had been stirred up by the Salvarsan treatment, ordered a spinal fluid test. It was negative, but Mabel would never know for sure.

On one occasion, Mabel and Tony were sitting with Brett and Frieda and D. H. Lawrence. He was ranting on against a decadent society, and said, "Only the doctors know the truth about these 'best people.'" They know that the rate of syphilis among them is enormous. They are rotten from it. The men have lost their manhood from it, the women their fertility. Our own best friends are filthy with it for all we know!"[56]

No one said anything. They went on eating bread and jam and drinking cocoa.

I had difficulty blending the horror of Mabel's secret with her writings in *Winter in Taos*. Her life up at the Big House sounded so healthy and idyllic. She describes the bounty of their little farm and cellars filled with potatoes and pumpkins, squash and fresh meat hanging in the cold room. Perhaps the powers of the land did in fact heal her. Perhaps her mindfulness of the sweetness of the daily life, the affections of her little rescued bulldog, Pooch, her horseback rides with Tony out onto the Pueblo lands, where he pointed out and taught her to identify the track of each wild animal, were actually heightened by the vein of darkness that now stained her life.

A Passion for Houses

"It seems an obvious thing to say," wrote Mabel. "Yet how many people know that beauty and reality in a house come from a sharp personal feeling for all the things in a house—and for a need to have them there, either for use or merely to live in through the eye?" She went on to say that she had never had any of her rooms just "arranged"[57]

She believed that our homes reflect our personalities and sometimes change noticeably year after year. I loved her description of her houses as "the shells of the soul in its progressive metamorphoses." It would not be long before a startling revelation of my own, would show me the validity of Mabel's observation.

Throughout her memoirs, Mabel repeatedly refers to her deep connection with the rooms she lived in. She was first influenced by the ugly and claustrophobic rooms of her childhood home, where the only thing which gave her pleasure were the little English Christmas figures on the wallpaper of her room. After her marriage to Edwin Dodge, she undertook a Renaissance-style restoration in the rooms of Villa Curonia in Florence, where she observed astutely, "In a lack of love I had tried to pass out of longing into materials."

"I knew quite well the kind of queen I wanted to be and the type of royal residence in which I would immolate myself. It would allow one to be both majestic and careless, spontaneous and picturesque, and yet always framed and supported by a secure and beautiful authenticity of background."[58]

Thus, Mabel decorated and furnished each room to reflect some aspect of her emotions. Her favorite room appears to have been the *Gran' Salone*.

"The way the light came in past the full golden red curtains, the way the logs burning behind the grill threw golden light on the dark oak floor, the glimpses of the Italian hills one caught from outside the loggia, framed between the pale stone columns…like the backgrounds in early Florentine paintings, firelight flickering on silver and bronze, somnolent great masses of flowers from the garden. There was a soothing magic in all this."

In Florence she was exquisitely aware of how the rooms we create also shape us. "The Villa Curonia loomed sumptuously about me, heavy, golden—carried so far towards perfection, it seemed important to me—a career in itself."[59]

White is a color associated with purity, freshness, innocence and new beginnings and when Mabel chose white on white for her Fifth Avenue apartment she would have been well aware of her craving for these qualities after all the emotional darkness of her final years in Florence

Later, her insights about the houses she lived in with Dodge are revealing. "In a lack of love I had tried to pass out of longing into materials—and out of my passion I had built my house. Now I was caught and entangled in it—now it was too powerful for me to tear myself out of, to go seeking mere stark delight.[60]

After the termination of her marriage to Dodge, when she'd met Maurice Sterne who would become her third husband, she discovered a different kind of setting, the country. Her response to the plain old farmhouse, Finney Farm, in Croton-on-Hudson, reveals a Mabel quite different from her public persona. Her response also foreshadows the feeling of finally finding her place, of coming home, which marked the creation, with Tony, of the house in Taos.

She found Finney Farm with Elizabeth Duncan, whose school Mabel had helped set up in Croton. The two women walked over from the school to the farm. The old white clapboard farmhouse moved her. "How peaceful it looked! The luxuriance of it all, the country opulence and wholesomeness were full of reassurance to me. How had I put up with my New York apartment for so long?"

Right then, she leased the farmhouse for two years.

"Finney Farm was always bright with sunlight and wood fires. In the big homely kitchen, there was always the smell of baking and roasting, of cinnamon and apples and hot coffee."[61]

As she writes about her rooms it's clear that she was exquisitely aware of how our rooms affect us, for example the harmony induced by fresh flowers. Phoebe Cottam had told me that, right up to the end, Mabel would always have whatever flowers were available from the garden. Phoebe remembered especially, the daffodils and Mabel frequently mentions vases full of freesias.

Building Mabel's Home

The Big House would be the first house that Mabel created from the ground up. Tony, working with men from the Pueblo, formed the adobe bricks from the earth, mixed with straw and water. The great beams and the stripped saplings of the ceilings, they cut and hauled from the slopes of the mountain. The plaster used for the interior walls and fireplaces was made from white earth, *tierra blanca,* and her friend and father of her new daughter-in-law, William Penhallow Henderson, fashioned the black and sienna tiles in the dining room, making the tiles out back of the building.

Mabel designed each tiny detail of the interior with an impeccable eye to the way light falls through each window and reflects the interior materials. The rooms are whimsical and playful. The entryways are arched in a variety of ways, each an individual. The fireplaces, with their noble proportions are precisely the right size for the room. There are no sharp or awkward angles, the rooms flow one to another. In the dining room, the *latillas* between the beams have been stained to echo the colors in a Navajo blanket; black, white, red the color of clay.

During the many times I sat in the Rainbow living room, I was always aware of the light. Never too bright, never gloomy. The way Mabel designed the windows, including a long one at the end of the room, placed lower than the usual height, and the materials used in every interior detail, to this day creates a soft welcoming intimacy downstairs. Upstairs, the mood changes, using the walls of windows as a way to blend with the mountains as well as take full advantage of the sunlight.

A Bowl of Lemons

One of my own earliest memories is of around age three, when my mother took me with her on the train to visit my aunt. When we arrived, she unlatched the gate and I followed her down a shady path to the front door. While she and my aunt greeted each other I looked around.

In the dining room on a well waxed table of dark wood, stood a blue china bowl filled with lemons. They were fresh from a tree in the garden and the sharp citrus tang of the lemons mixed with the smell of furniture wax penetrated my senses. Today, if I close my eyes I can still see the way the afternoon light, muted by dark burgundy velvet curtains, fell on that bowl of lemons.

Like Mabel, I was fascinated by the rooms around me. Mother told me that even as a small child I would embarrass her at friends' houses by rearranging things, even moving small pieces of furniture. I created the furnishings and colors, the objects in my own room until I was satisfied, and when I won a school prize for literature, I selected as my prize, a large glossy book on Japanese design.

David and I shared a passion for houses. Early on, we agreed that romantic old houses gave us more pleasure than stocks or other paper investments. We probably, to be more accurate, should have admitted that the romantic old houses were also in danger of crumbling into the ground on which they stood. Shortly after our marriage we had, based on our affection for Gerald Durrell's enchanting book, *My Family and Other Animals*, lived on the Greek island of Corfu for almost a year, working as free-lance writers.

We rented from George Varthis, and were delighted when he told us he had, as a young man, rented to the Durrells. The tiny charming villa, set in an olive grove leading down to its own half-moon beach, looked adorable. Painted what Durrell had referred to as "strawberry pink," there was one big room upstairs and one down, with a kitchen. The bathroom was upstairs. The builders had clearly completed the house in those hot summer months and considered heating unnecessary, so we bought a portable heater and dragged it upstairs and down, morning and evening.

Villa Mimosa, on a sunny day was entrancing. Corfu, unlike most of the Greek isles, is green. However, to be that lush, seductive green, it rains most of the winter and we, eager to escape the northern winter, arrived on our enchanted Greek isle in November. It was clear the house reflected our preference for romance over practicality, a tendency that has continued to affect our choice of homes.

When we returned from Greece, we discovered Edward House, a seventeen room Federal Colonial heap in northern Vermont. David's father's family were staunch Vermonters, his great-great-great grandfather, had built the eponymous Jonathan Elkins' tavern in Peacham in 1792.

Mabel believed in magic. When I think about all the coincidences which guided Mabel to Taos and the house on Morada Lane, there is an unmistakable sense of magic. One of my first encounters with a similar magic related to that house in Peacham. The summer I was eighteen, I worked as a housemaid at a resort in the Australian Alps. On Saturday nights staff were permitted to watch a movie with the guests. I recall Hayley Mills in a Walt Disney movie, *Summer Magic*. The house, overlooking rolling green meadows, was white clapboard, complete with a picket fence and lilacs.

Just three years later, when David and I were married in Peacham, in the small white-spired town church, Harvard historian, Crane

Brinton, who now owned the Jonathan Elkins Tavern, opened it to us for our reception. The house looked familiar. Remarkably, I recognized it as the house used in the filming of *Summer Magic*.

When we discovered Edward House, closer to the Canadian border, we threw ourselves into a restoration project which would surely have daunted even Mabel. Built in 1840, by the time we fell in love with the massive wooden doors and paneling of the library, even the contractor wasn't sure he could salvage it. But we had a vision and our faith rarely wavered.

We obsessed over that house until each room was fresh and welcoming. Over the years as we fell in love with other places including the Southwest, we indulged without reservation, our passion for houses. We agreed that the rooms had to "feel good," and were thrilled when friends felt at home.

The Hospital Birthing Room

This passion for houses served me well when my career in childbirth education took an interesting turn. When I graduated in Melbourne as a physiotherapist, my favorite part of the course had been the weeks at the Royal Women's Hospital working with midwives. Women in labor were encouraged to walk as long as they could in labor, refreshing themselves with sips of tea. As the moment of birth approached, we would help them onto their side, into the Sim's position, used to allow the baby to slide out and reduce the possibility of tearing. I enjoyed teaching pre-natal classes. My final exam report said, "Her voice is too soft for teaching but women will love her interested manner."

When I moved to North America, somehow I managed to transcend my soft voice and plunged wholeheartedly into the world of childbirth. My experiences convinced me that how a woman is treated in childbirth affects both her self-esteem and her interaction with her baby.

After ten months working as a general physiotherapist in the Canadian resort town of Kenora, 140 miles east of Winnipeg, I left for a position in Southampton, England. I never made it to England. In Montreal, I visited a friend who had had surgery at The Catherine Booth Hospital. I was sitting in the lobby when the director, or Major, came out of her office. She was talking with another woman. It turned out that the girl who taught the pre-natal classes had just left.

"I can do that," I said. They hired me. I was barely twenty years old and had never had a child. To be as close to the birth process as possible, without actually becoming pregnant, I moved into the hospital residence, managing to conceal my Siamese kitten in my room. On hand around the clock, I indulged my fascination with birth and was thrilled to accompany as many women as I could from my classes, through the births of their children. They taught me not only about the physical process but equally important about the complex emotional passage of each phase of labor.

The Birth of Mabel's Son

Shortly after her marriage to Karl Evans, Mabel miscarried and her doctor summoned a specialist to come and "take care of things." Her next pregnancy progressed to term and she enjoyed a feeling of being connected to nature.

All that changed with the birth itself. Back then, at the turn of the century, women did not receive any positive preparation for childbirth. The Biblical, "in sorrow thou shalt bring forth children" was the order of the day. If you were fortunate, female relatives or friends would comfort and support you during labor. No such comfort was available to Mabel.

When her waters broke and the "iron hand" of contractions gripped her, she did not appear to have any emotional support at all, least of all from her mother. In the fashion of the day, her doctor gave her chloroform for the pain Mabel described as "outrageous." Not surprisingly for a woman regaining consciousness, she felt no immediate connection to her baby and no effort appears to have been made to help the bonding process. As her son was taken by the nurse who would care for him, Mabel lay in bed trying to conceal her tears.

Looking back many years later when her son, John, was a grown man, Mabel reflected that though he had been right there with her throughout his first year, she'd never really known him.

The more women I accompanied in labor, the more I believed not just in preparing women with tools to reduce physical pain, but in the importance of emotional preparation for bonding with a new baby.

For the next seventeen years I worked with women and their families. In a supportive environment, women trust their bodies, and know how to give birth. The problem was that the hospital, with its labor beds and awkward move to a sterile delivery room which resembled a surgical operating theater, interfered with the normal process.

Take a woman with a normal labor, confine her to bed, hook her up to an intravenous drip and a fetal heart monitor, examine her internally at regular intervals, speed her labor up with artificial hormones and chances are she'll require an epidural anesthetic which increases the need for a whole chain of medical "interventions" up to and often including caesarean section. Intervention is a vicious circle. Research indicates that for the majority of women, the safest, easiest birth occurs when, instead of being confined to bed, the woman can walk around and change position. Back in my training days with the midwives that's exactly what was encouraged.

The birthing system in North America was changing, a wave that built from the action of a group of parents who were prepared to ask for what they wanted and expected to get it.

After a trip to Amsterdam, I was convinced that we somehow needed to change the philosophy of birthing. In Holland, birth was viewed as a normal process rather than something hazardous. True, there will always be a small percentage of women and their unborn babies for whom birth is potentially dangerous; the latest developments in high-risk care are completely justified in these situations.

The skill, I believe, in obstetrics, is to screen pregnancies carefully, giving those women at risk, the best in high-risk care, and using the art and science of midwifery for the majority of women. This was the secret of Holland's safe birth system. I had chosen to study Holland as it, along with Sweden, had the best statistical birth outcomes in the world for both mother and baby.

But how to change a philosophy? You can't suddenly walk into a labor-and-delivery suite and announce, birth is normal, out with the equipment. To begin with, you need women and their partners who are educated about the process of birth and are prepared to cope with pain by non-medical means such as positioning, walking, relaxation and emotional support. And you need a staff also prepared to help parents cope in this way.

After much consideration, it seemed to me that the most effective way to change the philosophy was with a physical environment such as the Dutch one-room system.

By this time I'd been invited to set up a course in obstetrics for second and third year students at McGill University's School of Physical and Occupational Therapy. This position opened doors. I approached each of the large Montreal hospitals to discuss a new approach. The answer was no. But once an intention is strong, it creates an energy which builds. The National Film Board of Canada was making a documentary called "An Unremarkable Birth," the technical term for normal birth. Designed for television, the 52 minute film followed one of the couples from my classes who, because the father had not been permitted to attend the birth of his first child, chose with the second child, to give birth in the labor room with privacy and no unnecessary intervention.

As part of the new dialogue between parents and hospital staff, they were filming a meeting at McGill's Hosmer House, in the School of Physical Therapy. That meeting would change the history of birthing.

After the filming, Morrie Gelfand, Chief of Obstetrics at the Jewish General Hospital, said to me, "I'd like you to come in and set up what you're talking about, this new room idea. We have an empty suite at the end of labor and delivery. You could start right away. Let me know what you need."

I was excited by his offer, and in 1978, set up what would become the first Hospital Birthing Room in North America. Starting with two connecting rooms at the end of a row of conventional labor rooms, the best use of the area was clearly a bedroom and a sitting room where family and friends could visit and offer love and support. A room which resembled home as much as possible would reduce fear and the resulting tension that we know increases pain.

The groundwork for the change in philosophy was preparation of both parents and staff. As this gained momentum, on a sunny summer morning, David, and I, now parents of a baby daughter, made a trip to Pascal's Furniture Warehouse. We chose a big brass double bed that invited the father to snuggle with his partner in labor, one big enough for both parents to relax in during the first breastfeeding after birth.

Then we chose a chocolate brown sofa-bed and a sturdy rocking chair for the sitting room. We added a wooden coffee table, a braided rug, soft brown and yellow flowered wallpaper, deep golden yellow curtains and a fluffy, floral comforter.

The conventional labor rooms with their pale greens, whites and metal beds felt cold and uninviting. We know now that whatever produces fear and tension also interrupts the normal progress of labor.

What happened? The room was not just a pretty place. By forbidding the use of high-risk interventions in the Birthing Room, the philosophy of normal birthing could be developed and protected. Mobility was an essential ingredient. If a woman walks and changes her position frequently, labor can progress as much as 36% faster than if she is confined to bed. Interventions which, back then, were routine, such as a "just in case" intravenous drip and fetal heart monitors which require the woman to remain in bed, have been found to increase the risk of fetal heart distress. Thus, medical staff attending women in the Birthing Room agreed to avoid these procedures. If abnormalities were detected, women could easily be transferred to a regular labor and delivery room.

It was fascinating to watch the effects of a change in environment. The first was privacy. In the regular labor rooms, interns and residents thought nothing of entering without knocking, of treating the woman as a nameless patient. Frequently the bed was placed so that the woman couldn't even see who was coming in. In this new environment staff spontaneously knocked before entering much the way they would if they were visitors in the woman's house. We positioned the bed so that the woman could see anyone who entered.

Something wonderful was happening. As the atmosphere became more home-like, parents and staff began to laugh together and share personal information. Not surprisingly, the outcome reflected the changes. The results of a lengthy research project revealed that not only was the Birthing Room as safe as the conventional labor-delivery room, but the rate of medical interventions such as episiotomy, a surgical cut made to enlarge the vaginal opening, dropped. Equally important was the overall conclusion that women and their partners felt more relaxed and confident in the home-like environment.

Common sense? Yes, but often in short supply. We were witnessing an amazing breakthrough. Two of my books, *The Rights of the Pregnant Parent* and *The Birth Report*, with the publicity they generated, helped accelerate the changes. Everyone was talking about Birthing Rooms and over the next five years I was invited to present the concept to hospitals across North America. Today, virtually every hospital in the country has a Birthing Room, indeed my grandchildren, Madeleine and Parker were born in a hospital Birthing Room which grew from my consultation.

Work with the Birthing Rooms rekindled my long-term fascination with the way our physical environment affects us and, like Mabel Dodge Luhan, I became increasingly aware of this connection. Later, as I read and reread Mabel's account of her son's birth and her lack of feeling for him in his first year, I wondered how her experience might have differed had she had a Birthing Room available. It was apparent from everything she'd written how sensitive she was to her physical surroundings.

Mabel's Rooms

Mabel wrote in *Intimate Memories*, "...the houses I have lived in have shown the natural growth of a personality struggling to become individual, growing through all degrees of crudity to a greater sophistication and on to simplicity they are like the shells of the soul in its progressive metamorphoses—faithfully revealing the form of the life they sheltered until they were outgrown and discarded."

If we take this into account and follow Mabel from the ornate and exquisitely decorated Villa Curonia, to the white on white of 23 Fifth Avenue where she longed for new beginnings, to friendly old Finney Farm and finally to the house she and Tony built at the top of Morada Lane in Taos, the clues to Mabel's passage can be found in the floor plan, the arrangement of furniture in her rooms, the colors she selected, the objects she collected.

By the time I visited the Big House, as Phoebe Cottam told me, Dennis Hopper had removed most of the fine wood, the acqua and yellow silken French and Italian furniture. The emerald and magenta pillows had long fallen apart, perhaps hastened by the small paws of Pooch and Friends. The drawers full of memorabilia Mabel brought with her from house to house had disappeared. These are vividly described in Mabel's memoirs.

After completing my novel about illness, *The Loneliness of Angels*, I embarked on a cheerier voyage which grew from both my childhood passion for houses and my work with the hospital Birthing Room that showed how our surroundings affect us.

One sticky hot day in Montreal, I was unloading some groceries from the car when a friend pulled up. It was Debbi, who ran the kennel where I boarded my dogs, a place where I knew they'd be well cared for when I traveled. She and her partner Marcello, provided a convenient pick-up service and the moment they arrived my dogs began to bark and wag their tails. They couldn't wait to climb into the van and be off on an adventure of their own.

I hadn't seen Debbi for a while. I knew she was involved with Greyhound Rescue, finding homes for discarded racing dogs.

"Hi Debbie, how's it going?"

Instead of her customary cheerfulness, Debbi gave me a worried look.

"Not so good. You know how I've always wanted to swim and work with wild dolphins? Well, I've got my chance down in Florida. And Marcello wants to sail around the world. We put the kennel up for sale, along came a buyer and I bought a house down in Florida. Now the kennel sale's fallen through and I'm supposed to sign for the new house in a month. I don't know what I'm going to do."

Though I was distressed that the people my dogs loved were leaving the pet boarding business, the words that popped out of my mouth were, "How would you feel if I came and took a look at the kennel?"

"Sure, if you have any ideas that would be terrific."

"How'd tomorrow afternoon be?"

"Great."

The lobby of the kennel was, as usual, friendly and attractive, with big posters of their latest greyhounds up for adoption on the board. I wandered through the cattery where a handful of free-range cats lounged in the sun. The grooming room was attractive, pink towels covering the tables.

The moment I approached the back door I knew I was onto something. There were two doors, an inner and an outer. I opened the first door. The area between the doors was dim and dingy. In a corner leaned a rusty hand mower with some old dead leaves caught in the blades. On the wall beside it were cobwebs. The outer door looked weary, with its peeling paint and rusty hardware. Beyond this door stretched the fenced-in field where they exercised the dogs.

What if this tired old door was precisely that? What if it were interpreted literally? A door into the world which is rusted and not able to open to its maximum? What if this compromised exit prevented Debbi's exit into the world?

On a hunch, I suggested to Debbi that they make this area as sparkling and attractive as the rest of the kennel. The next weekend they got rid of the lawnmower, cleared out the area and painted the door.

In two weeks a new buyer appeared, someone they had known for years and trusted. This time the sale went through and they both set off to follow their dreams.

I wasn't sure that my suggestions had made a difference, but if they had, I was happy to help. I forgot about the kennel and went back to my writing.

Then my phone started to ring. The quick sale after the changes I'd suggested, caused Debbi to think I had some hidden talent. She gave my number to a slew of her friends. "Debbi told us what happened at the kennel," they'd say. "Could you take a look at my apartment? Or house? Or studio?"

I didn't view myself as qualified, until I discussed my feelings with my daughter. "Don't be silly, Mummy," she said. "You've spent most of your life designing Birthing Rooms. You'd be pretty slow if by now you don't understand how rooms affect us."

Put in those words, I decided to plunge in and apply to private homes, what I'd learned in hospitals. This new direction opened to me a whole new an exciting world. My winters in Taos had banished bronchitis and, inspired by Mabel, I was ready to burst into something new and exciting.

Shortly after my decision, I was fortunate to have an experience that showed me, beyond a doubt, that the rooms we live in not only *affect* us, they also *reflect* us.

House Whispering

It was snowing lightly the day I arrived at Marie-Therese's home. The apartment was in a high-end complex on the outskirts of town, complete with pools, tennis courts, shopping center and health club. A vigilant doorman took the license of my car and ushered me into seemingly miles of mirrored hallways and hushed elevators.

I had decided early on to ask my clients not to tell me anything about themselves. This was important to me.

"As far as I'm concerned, my clients are Snow White and the seven Dwarves," I'd joke at our initial phone call. "I don't want to know how many people live here, who they are or what they do."

Marie-Therese's entrance was tastefully decorated with expensive furnishings, carefully chosen artwork, lots of healthy plants and big windows which on sunny days must have bathed the whole apartment in light. She showed me the coat closet and went back to a telephone conversation.

"Think of me as a sort of friendly ghost," I'd suggested. "Just go ahead and do what you'd do normally. I'm going to snoop and creep and when I'm finished we can walk through and discuss it all." If the truth be known, I always consider anyone who invites a stranger into her or his house to snoop and creep, rather brave!

I had trained myself to focus on a central clue. It had always happened before, the one small piece of evidence which invited me to unravel the secrets of what was really happening in my client's life. Without knowing quite why, I headed down a hallway to what was obviously the master bedroom, fine bed, lovely linens and a view of the city.

My eyes were immediately drawn to a corner, however. On the wall hung an oil painting of an old house. It was clearly the work of a talented artist. The wooden roof was sagging, the house in apparent decay. Snow covered part of the roof and the surrounding landscape of bare trees made me shiver. Though I loved the snow falling at the Taos Pueblo on Christmas Eve, the snow of cities reminds me of those years of bronchitis, propped up in bed staring out at the icy rooftops.

A few feet from the painting was a piece of sculpture, a bronze of a young dancer, poised on one leg, the other stretched behind.

Suddenly it came to me what was going on in Marie-Therese's life, the central theme, the challenge. I must confess I was somewhat reluctant to share my thoughts wit her. What if I were wrong? Don't be silly, I told myself, you didn't choose to do this, it chose you. Either you have the gift or you don't. If you don't, it's better to find out before you mess up someone's life.

Marie-Therese made us tea. After some general information about what I'd found in the apartment, I jumped right in. "The central issue right now is about your relationships. There appear to be two relationships. The first is represented by the painting in your bedroom, the one of the old house in winter; the second by the sculpture of the bronze dancer. It's as though the first relationship is decaying, the emotions frozen, while the second is the dancer on one leg, poised in flight."

The woman, strong and impressive, looked stunned. We sat at the table in silence. Outside, a surprise early-fall snow continued to drift by the window. Then, recovering, she said slowly.

"What you've said is completely accurate. I've been having a relationship for years with a man who's not available to marry me and it's really not going anywhere. He's much older than I am and now his health's going downhill. Then about six months ago I met a terrific younger man, but like you said with the dancer, he's poised to fly off, he's not ready to commit."

"I keep going round and round the same old stuff in my mind. Right now I can't concentrate on my career. I just want to get clear about where my relationships are going."

Marie-Therese called me some time later. "I decided to sell the painting and the sculpture as well. I can't believe how things have changed. You'll laugh, but I have to tell you, I have all these men calling me, asking me out, but right now I just want to get on with my work. I'm writing a book and have a publisher who's interested."

My session with the old house and the dancer brought up a lot of questions. Had Marie-Therese been affected by her choice of artwork, or had she unconsciously selected art which reflected what was going on in her life? And if this were so, then perhaps every tiny thing we choose to surround ourselves with tells a tale, expresses, if you will, our inner blueprint.

Our Houses: Sanctuaries or Prisons?

Mabel had written in her *Intimate Memories,* "I have never, thank God, regarded things as merely inanimate. They have always lived for me or else I did not have them about."

In Florence, however, she had second thoughts about her carefully constructed opulence. "I sometimes lay in my green-and-gold bed guarded by the four crusty lions, and I thought: "Myself and another just lying on the bare earth—instead of this. Would it be worth it? And some part of me leaped, pressing against the barriers, yearning outward towards the world, crying, "Let's go!" but another part sank deeper into feathers—decreeing I should stay in my beautiful shell. So to protect and comfort ourselves do we build our prisons."[69]

Only on her return to New York, at Finney Farm in Croton, did she experience pleasure away from the city, in the simple farmhouse, enjoying the land itself.

I returned to Taos each winter, with a new confidence as my bronchitis became a thing of the past. As my work with houses developed, I began to develop a program which allowed me to blend my three passions, writing, paying attention to what our homes say about us, and birth.

Mabel had observed that it was impossible to be cheerful and optimistic if one's house was a mess. In a similar way I'd observed that it was difficult to feel relaxed and confident giving birth in a surgical atmosphere. I'd been fortunate to spend years watching the extraordinary way parents and attending staff were affected by physical surroundings. My new experiences with houses gave me the opportunity to figure out how we could use this knowledge to empower our daily lives.

The workshops which resulted, centered on a method of journaling our relationship with each home we have ever lived in. We revisit and look at what has formed us and what we in turn have created. Mabel's insight that we create our houses to " protect and comfort us" but as we live in them they become our prisons seemed to me particularly powerful.

When I first read these words it was not clear to me what exactly she meant. However, following my work with the images of the old house and the bronze dancer, her words had new meaning.

Do we, beginning in childhood, absorb familiar patterns which are reflected in the family house? Do we carry these patterns with us throughout life, selecting homes that continue these patterns? After I'd worked with many homes it was apparent that in addition to our gifts, our homes also carry old patterns which may limit us. Most of us are aware of our limitations, but how do we transform them into opportunities?

These patterns may be changed through life experience or inner awareness. Sometimes, however, they may be locked in for a full lifetime. The workshops developed from my initial work with the hospital Birthing Rooms, appeared to offer a way to consciously change old patterns and align our homes with current goals.

I was grateful to the participants who generously shared with me the changes in their lives in the months and years following their house explorations. They taught me that it is in fact, possible to mindfully create homes of harmony and beauty which comfort and protect without imprisoning us.

Mabel: Privileged or Deprived?

One afternoon after re-reading Mabel's observation about our houses becoming our prisons, I took a cup of tea into the sunny greenhouse, stretched out on my deck chair and admired the big, healthy red geraniums. As I sipped my green tea I thought about Mabel's life.

Outwardly, she appeared to have had it all—mansions, men and money. Inwardly it was a different story. The unloved child of a loveless marriage, at a time when divorce was not acceptable, she watched her parents trapped together in unhappiness. She was exquisitely sensitive to her surroundings and clearly this unhappiness was reflected in the rooms around her, which threatened to become her first "prison." Mabel was however, strong and resilient. With no affection shown her and without role models, she forged ahead, trusting in her own "inner force."

Girls of her day were expected to either marry or become what was derisively referred to as "old maids," so it is not surprising that Mabel accepted the marriage trap set by Karl Evans. She had no illusions. "When I was twenty-one I was married—the passive, the truly female experience."

Children were an expected part of marriage and reliable contraception was not readily available. The combination of a traumatic birth to a thirteen pound baby for whom she felt no affection, her father's death from syphilis and her husband's death in a shooting accident, all within a short period of time, surely created significant trauma. The depression, or melancholy, which stalked her throughout her next two marriages, recurred shortly after the marriage certificate was signed. Evans literally trapped her into marrying him. Certainly she described the feelings of 'entrapment" which followed her second and third marriages to both Dodge and Sterne.

Yet even had she not been literally trapped, that first time, could an intelligent woman who craved an identity of her own, have felt fulfilled by marriage back then? If you had money, you spent your days supervising the servants, fussing about household management. If you did not have money, you spent your days as a servant, being bossed around.

Between times you were pregnant and either supervised the children's nannies or cared for your offspring yourself. If you were lucky, you threw yourself into these roles with gusto and did not expect much else. Husbands were not expected to pay attention to women's feelings. As the first world war surged through Europe, men left their women and gathered together, drawn by the romance of battle.

Mabel wrote, "Men do not really mind a woman's agony and loneliness; it gives them their independence and security and they like the women's jealousy too."[62] Mabel's struggle to cope with melancholy was relentless. She tried everything from Christian Science to occultism and psychoanalysis. What might have happened to her without her writing?

At that time, even the most rebellious young women could not entirely escape their conditioning. Mabel's expectations of herself as a muse to men were a product of the "new woman" in transition. What is surprising is the bold and exciting way she launched herself to connect and inspire the great minds and artistic talents of the day. When she was young, she was told by a family friend, "You have a brain, Mabel. You have a brain," as though this were something startling to find in a woman.

Mabel had a horror of being idle. She describes feeling the dread of having nothing to do as "so heavy, so desolate and so painful that nothing is quite so hard to bear." From an early age, she wanted to be useful. As a child, the only women she saw come and go with freedom were the nurses who came and went to minister to her dying father.

"I'm going to be a hospital nurse," I announced. In those days a hospital nurse represented the most desirably situated woman alive!"[63]

It is clear that her relationships with men, at least until she met Tony Luhan, gave her little real affection and pleasure. At one point, watching her son emerge from the surf with Edwin Dodge, she makes a startling comment, "I decided that I really hated men anyway."[64] Did Mabel, I wondered, actually hate men, or was it that all the male/female relationships of the day were stacked in favor of the man? He was free to sleep around, to bury himself in his work, to do as he pleased with few social constraints.

In spite of the turbulent relationships which resulted, Mabel had no difficulty attracting men. She described her natural empathy. "I have always been myself, and at the same time, someone else, always able to be the other person, feel with him, think his thoughts." While men responded to this empathy, they rarely appeared to return it.

A key to what has been described as Mabel's "elusive personality" was perhaps revealed when she wrote, "I learned very early to talk to people only of the things they knew and liked and never to try to tell them all that I carried locked up I me. In this way, from the first, I always seemed a different person to all the different people I ever knew."[65]

The pressures of the day propelled the emerging "new woman'" inexorably to men and marriage. Some, like writers, Neith Boyce and Hutchins Hapgood, experimented with "open marriage," but that was not without problems, as Hutchins explored in *Story of a Lover*. In her wonderful book, *Ladies of the Canyons*, Lesley Poling-Kempes describes the talented and often financially independent women who carved their niche in the Southwest and all too often, like Carol Stanley, who built Ghost Ranch, then sold it to Arthur Pack, sacrificed their peace of mind as well as their money in ill-fated marriages.

Perhaps it was inevitable that relationships at this time appeared to involve issues of push and pull as women tried to redefine their roles and men responded in traditional ways. While in Florence, Mabel wrote, "My life was completely inactive. I rarely left the place and then only in a carriage the few times I went shopping or to call for Edwin at the tennis court, for I had to do this occasionally to make sure that he was not playing with some woman or girl, but only with men, as I had made him promise me."[66]

I thought about my work with women in childbirth. In the 1970s, childbirth, surely an area undeniably female, was dominated by men. The obstetrician, almost always a man, was god. Even as birth approached, it was the male doctor, not the woman, who was said to "deliver" her child. It would take the next decade for the birthing culture to recognize childbirth as a woman's domain.

My obstetrician friend, Murray Enkin, one of the pioneers of changes in hospital birth, once quipped that "the M. Deity won't get down from his throne until women get up from their knees." Once this was underway, acknowledging the right of a father to attend the birth of his child would create, for the first time in North America, a man's participation in the rearing of his child.

This was a breakthrough which would bring down old barriers and clear the way for new ways of parenting. At the time Mabel gave birth, this part of feminism had scarcely been articulated.

Mabel and Tony

It's clear that Mabel's connection to Nature was central to her "inner force." Once, Maurice Sterne asked what made her so fearless and she replied, "Nature." Several times she refers to the pleasure she feels lying face down on the warm earth, feeling the "earth energies," and some of her happiest experiences revolve around the times she and Tony shared out on the land.

Perhaps this connection with nature was part of the key to her long marriage to Tony Luhan? In spite of the syphilis which had driven a wedge between them shortly after their marriage, their love continued to grow. Unlike her succession of former lovers and husbands, Tony did not appear to need Mabel as his Muse. Richly steeped in the traditions of the Pueblo, he would go off by himself into that world that Mabel sensed but could not share. When he returned to the Big House, however, they did share the small events of the day in a way that seems to have drawn them close.

"Every once in a while, after the oats are up, you'll see Tony walking around the nearby field after sundown, peering down, trying to see signs of the new alfalfa. When I see him doing that, I go over and join him, for it's a heavenly thing to walk about in the early June fields after the sun has set; the earth is still warm and the air is full of scent of flowers, and the wild birds are settling down after the sweet excitement they have been fluttering in all day, feeding the small new birds in the nests."[67]

Frieda Lawrence on their first meeting, speculated that Tony was Mabel's rock. The couple had only been together five years then and Mabel was uncertain of this description. Twelve years later, however, Mabel agreed. "He seems like a rock; more than that, a mountain, that will support all the weight I can put on him. Nothing can really hurt a woman who has a man like this, to give her moral and emotional support. We could lose our houses and our horses, our friends, our health and our strength, but as long as we are together, we are immune from essential loss."[68]

Mabel at Home

Creating the Big House with Tony allowed Mabel, for the first time, to build her home from the ground up, exactly as she chose. Built on the edge of the sacred lands, of the earth itself, the house blended Tony's pueblo knowledge with her sensitivity to beauty and light. If our homes both affect and reflect us, then the welcoming, nurturing Big House surely was healing to Mabel and to all those who visited. As the years went by, her enjoyment of her home swelled to fill her memoirs.

Alone one evening she wrote,

"It really isn't worth it, I thought, to live here in this solitude, shut in by the winter, when everyone has gone somewhere else and is having an interesting time! But alas! I remembered I was here because I chose to be, and that no other kind of time anyone was having meant a thing to me, compared with my life, the way I had built it here. This was best for me, this home in the valley, where my work stretches out far ahead of me."[70]

Ultimately, Tony provided the solid, reliable and undemanding relationship Mabel had never had. Now she was free to write, to invite her friends, to simply live her life surrounded by a place she loved deeply. Periodically she and Tony traveled. She did at one point return to New York and attempt to resurrect her salon, but times had changed and so had she and she returned to Taos where, towards the end, she appeared satisfied to hang out with Frieda and Brett, worrying at times about where Tony might be. At the end of *Winter in Taos,* when he comes home after such an episode, Mabel cries to him,

> "Oh, Tony! I was so afraid something had happened to you. Why were you so late?" His face looked so smooth and benevolent as he put his kind hand on my shoulder.
> "What can happen? I wish you not worry like that. Why you frightened like that?"
> "Such a night—the storm—"
> Tony replied, "Don't you know the moon is shining?" he said smiling and he pulled the curtain back from the window to show me.[71]

Mabel's Girls: Free to Create

I met Carolynn Rafman several years after I began to winter in Taos. She was strolling down Morada Lane from Mabel's, notebook in hand. I was heading to Caffé Tazza, so we walked together. We were delighted to discover we both lived in Montreal and had spent much of our professional lives working at McGill University, I teaching childbirth education, she doing research on aging.

A few evenings later as we chopped vegetables for dinner at my little house, we discussed Mabel's legacy.

Carolynn, attracted first to Taos by Mabel's book, *Edge of Taos Desert*, had taken a workshop with Sas Colby, who offered journeys in personal exploration via many different approaches to mixed media.

For the next twenty five years, Carolynn would spend part of each summer helping with the workshops at Mabel's, making friends with a group of women who dubbed themselves, Mabel's Girls.

"I was initially drawn to Mabel's by her writing," Carolynn told me as she chopped carrots for our stir-fry. "And part of the reason I've kept coming back, apart from the workshops and my friendships here, is the very strong sense of place. One of the first workshops I took was one on Sacred Space. After that I wanted to spend more time in the house, wanted to spend more time getting to know people. Then friendships developed. I used to bring a friend, or cousin or my daughters, but once my youngest turned seventeen they didn't want to come any more, although they'd loved it, they had their own lives. I'm more independent now, I come on my own with just my dog, Tara, a New Mexico rescue.

"George and Susan Otero owned the house back then and they invited me to work behind the desk in reception. At that time it was still the old-fashioned reception system, before computers.

"For some reason I never use the front entrance at the top of the lane when I arrive at Mabel's, I always come up the stairs. The moment I cross the *acequia* I have that sense of sacred space, closed off from the rest of the world. I've had this from the beginning and many of the people who come to Mabel's feel this. It's almost as though we're in this bubble, Mabel's bubble.

"When I first started working at reception, it was still a bed and breakfast and one of my jobs was to set the dining room for breakfast. Well, not long after I started work I remember going from the reception area which is right under the sunroom, crossing the living room and going down the few stairs into the dining room.

"The dining room was a dark, empty, pregnant space. I had to cross the room to get things from the kitchen at the back and when I went into the kitchen it felt full of spirits, very strong spirits in there. It didn't feel malevolent, but it was something I hadn't felt before, so I didn't know whether to be fearful or not. I'd never had that experience before I went to New Mexico."

As Carolynn and I finished eating our stir-fry, and we returned to our discussion of our times at Mabel's, she reflected,

"Mabel's opened for me that sense of connection with the other, the understanding that place can hold so many spirits. I think it's because Mabel entertained so many people in that dining room. Now I just love to go in there. Every day when we have our meals, I'm always thinking about the many people who've passed through, were entertained, were entertaining and had wonderful food, always wonderful food."

A few years later, Carolynn and I got together for tea at my house in Montreal. It was early fall and though the days were still warm, the evenings had an icy nip. She had just returned from Taos and I was beginning to plan my customary winter getaway to 220 Morada Lane. In preparation, I was re-reading *Winter In Taos*.

"I think everyone who goes to Mabel's is influenced by her through the house she created," Carolynn told me. "There's something very special there, the way the adobe feels so calm, the way the doorways and windows are, the way she designed it, she was able to capture some sort of energy that stays in the home, very warm and welcoming, especially for women. There's something about Mabel's room, it's as though her spirit reaches out and inspires you to be yourself. All of us who come to the workshops, we all believe that Mabel brought us here and we give thanks for the opportunity to be in her house."

We sipped our tea and looked out over the city. The sky was a pale grey and the maple trees in the gardens were turning crimson. Soon the snow would claim this northern city. I felt the now familiar pull of the Southwest with its dry sparkling air and brilliant sunshine. One morning soon I'd hear the calls of Canada geese heading south in their V formation.

"You know some of Mabel's Girls swear she's actually appeared to them and sometimes there's a faint whiff of cinnamon, " Carolynn told me. "I've smelled that too. I love cinnamon."

"Yes, Mabel always did love cinnamon," I replied thinking of her description of Finney Farm, which always smelled of baking and roasting, apples, cinnamon and coffee.

"When I started going to Taos," continued Carolynn, "I heard a lot about Mabel's writing being criticized and underappreciated. I assumed that's a carry-over about women's writing in a man's world, but I love her books, she draws you right along. Some of the books that talk about Mabel tend to focus more on her as an impresario than on her own writing. You hear all these stories about Mabel and D. H. Lawrence and Frieda.

"Sometimes I feel that Mabel was misread. I was looking at a photo of her and I had the feeling she just wanted to be herself. In that photo it was as though she was saying, I'm really just a simple girl trying to expand my horizons. She never seemed jaded.

"When I went to Taos I had been through an emotionally turbulent time. I really identified with that northeast closed mentality that Mabel grew up in and the southwest seemed so wide open and expansive. Mabel was a gateway for me into a whole other life. My time at her house opened my life into a new realm of possibility. It's been a terrific place for me to move on from "motherhood." I know the work we do with Sas Colby has enriched my life, the multi-media artwork, the collages, the poetry. I've seen big changes in myself, opening up with the journaling and the art, exploring my creative self that had been dormant before I came to Mabel's.

"Part of the reason I keep coming back is Mabel's and part is the land itself. The mountain. She used to have a view of the mountain from the sunroom, but now in summer you don't get the same view she writes about, you have to go behind the house to see the great expansive view. Every year with Sas we've taken a walk from the morada out to the cross and that's where I have this incredible sense of the mountain and that's what draws me back to Taos, it's the mountain. Is the mountain going to welcome me back again? There's some sort of magical half-life when I go there, it's something I don't really understand, but I know when I'm there things just work, I meet people, things fall into place, there are no difficulties, I don't have any bad experiences. When I return there I heave a sigh of relief."

As our tea time drew to a close, Carolynn said, "When I was a young girl I read Thomas Moore and I used to love Utopian fiction. In high school we were asked to write down what we wanted from life and I wrote that I wanted to find Utopia. After years back and forth to Taos, I've realized that for me, Utopia is a place where women feel free to create. That's what Mabel has given us."

Mabel's Girls: A Safe Place

Some winters later I had a chance to sit and talk with Judy Jordan up at Mabel's. Judy worked as docent to the growing number of year-round visitors to the house.

"I first came out here from Brooklyn, New York and now I've worked here five years. I attended Natalie Goldberg workshop," she told me. "And I was staying off-property. I didn't really get the house much the first time I came and then, living in Taos, I didn't really have contact with the house. Then when I went back east I started dreaming about Taos. The dreams were about buildings I hadn't even been into. I decided to put my house up for sale. It sold in one week and I moved out here.

"The second time I came I stayed here, at Mabel's. It felt a safe place to stay as a single woman. It felt a very peaceful place and I enjoyed it enormously. I didn't know much about Mabel back then, I was resettling, so I had other things pulling me.

"Now I work at the front desk and do the tours. We have a lot of people who just want to come by for the house. We've had a number of people from England and Germany and France and some from Australia. We've also had some Japanese visitors who came because they were very pro-Lawrence. There is a huge popularity in Japan for D. H. Lawrence.

"Mabel changed a lot over her lifetime," she continued. "She came out here in search of something, it was almost a mid-life crisis. It's always been hard to pin Mabel down and I think it was this willingness to change that has produced an elusiveness. " She thought for a while. "This was the first house she actually built and owned. She just decorated the Villa Curonia and twenty-three Park Avenue.

"Mabel was a trailblazer for her time, she managed to kick over the traces of that upper middle class childhood in Buffalo. These days, all her marital experiences wouldn't seem extraordinary, but she still continues to inspire us. I think it has a very large part to do with this house that she built."

When Judy described her feelings each time she arrived at Mabel's, her words echoed Carolynn's.

"The moment you walk over the bridge," said Judy, "it's a different world up here and sometimes when I come up to work I feel it so strongly. There is a grounding for this piece of land that feels extraordinary. It was built from the earth, it was designed to be part of the earth and it was designed to be in harmony with the sacred mountain and its lands. There's not really any place like it. People come here to visit the house and right away they get it.

"We're very lucky," she continued. "The family foundation that owns the property now has a very nurturing spirit towards it. The house always smells welcoming, of warmth and the smell of baking. We're very much a living entity, we're not a museum."

We discussed Mabel's writing and the impact it has had. "I think Mabel was a good writer," said Judy. "It's interesting because she's never been as recognized as other writers of her time, but there seems to be a growing swell of interest now in the time and in Mabel. We sold enormous numbers of her books this summer, people come to the house, they get enraptured with her story and they want to read more about her. The part of her writing I most enjoy is her reactions to the landscape and to her life here, she really enjoyed this crazy rustic life. When you think about it, it's amazing that she fit right in, from the Villa Curonia to this."

"Yes," I recalled. "When her mother came for a rare visit, Mabel worried that she would find the house jerrybuilt and run-down!"

We laughed.

Judy continued. "My perception of Mabel's personality is that it was complicated beyond belief. I think she was very much misunderstood. People think of her as being this rich dilettante but I don't think she was that because when you read her books you see how perceptive and sensitive she actually was. She really delved a lot into the human psyche. She did regard herself as having been sent to be a muse, there are so many quotes about that in Lois Rudnick's books."

A Place to Meet Yourself

A group of visiting women arrived at the desk. They were enthusiastic and for the next twenty minutes Judy answered their questions.

After they left, we sat down in the comfortable living room and Judy continued.

"Mabel had a vision of herself with the movers and shakers of the world and indeed she did move and shake the world around her; from the arts to the political world. One thing which is important to all of us who work here today is that while we may not attract the movers and shakers, we do provide what Mabel wished, which was a retreat for people to come, not just for the overnight conferences, but you can come and just stay here. It's kept purposefully low key. It's a place where you can meet yourself if you dare.

"I find the mountain a very compelling entity," she told me as we chatted about living in Taos. "This summer I was privileged to have a direct view of it from where I was living in El Prado. I could look out my window while I was washing dishes and look at the mountain. It felt very peaceful and looked very lush because I had an *acequia* which runs all year, about ten feet from the house. It was a real gift. I'd get up at dawn and watch the sun come up over the foothills and it was wonderful to be so close to the Pueblo land."

We finished by discussing Mabel's later years.

"When Mabel left the Big House," said Judy, "and moved across the road, her life changed. Part of that had to do with aging and ill health. She had health problems throughout her life and went back east several times for various operations. And at some point in aging you simply start to slow down. The house across the lane is much smaller than this and the upkeep of this house is expensive. All those parties she used to give! After the war all that changed."

"Mabel and Tony certainly had their ups and downs, but it was a true love story. These were two totally different people from two totally different worlds.

"My experience in Taos," Judy concluded, "has been extremely varied. Taos rips you open, it exposes you and if there are some lessons you haven't learned it teaches them to you. Some of it's been very difficult and it's given me a lot of growth."

Painting Intuitively

Recently, my friend, Katrin Themlitz stayed at Mabel's for a ten day painting experience taught by Michele Cassou. Called Creativity Rediscovered, most of the participants returned year after year, from as far away as the U.K. Cassou teaches The Point Zero Method of painting purely by intuition, designed to lead into "the wild, untamed place within us where there are no judgments or rules." No experience was required, just the desire to create naturally and spontaneously.

"The goal was not to create a product," Katrin told me, "but to connect with the intuitive flow. It's not about the image, the rule is you don't look at your painting or other peoples' paintings. We were encouraged to begin in the unknown and trust that 'it' would find its way. Nothing to figure out and resolve, something will occur to you next. Carl Jung said you cannot have two masters. Create a product or follow intuitive flow. If we do not get used to the unfamiliar, we become calcified with what we know."

Katrin continued. "The universe breathes a sigh of relief when you put paintbrush to paper and let your hand find its way. What we paint is what we don't know about ourselves. By putting paint to paper, we discover the stream of creativity that wants to take care of ourselves.

"We shared our meals in the dining room or, weather permitting, outside on the patio. Because most of the women were returns, it was as though they were meeting for an annual reconnection with themselves that nurtured their lives deeply throughout the year. There was lots of laughter and the knowing that hard things that had happened would be digested by the creative energy nurtured in this workshop. At the end the participants organized a play and a poetry showcase."

"I took several walks to the cemetery and the nearby church. There were many graves of young children. The church was shuttered with the big cross standing in front of Taos Mountain to the north and the sacred lands off-limits to non-natives. It seemed to me that worlds collide on the edge of this desert, the church like a ship on the ocean, holding up the cross at its bow, shipwrecked and washed ashore by ancient waves, like thought, frozen, as it forgets to be curious about life. Mabel's house stands on the edge of this desert where newer worlds appear to collide silently and more ancient and forgotten worlds emerge to make us whole again. It's as though ideas become less fixed, the universe sighs in relief and breathes once again.

"I've always thought that New Mexico is a kind of portal, a place where the veils are thin, and other worlds emerge to be felt.

"Mabel's house fascinated me. From the cobblestoned courtyards to painted and carved doors, each shaped differently, inviting a unique kind of energy to enter each room. I felt compelled to draw those shapes.

"There was this endless sense of wonder about all the people who had been drawn to Mabel's. What drew them here? Something beyond words, for sure. I also noticed the many fireplaces inside and out, where people gather for conversation, contemplation, or just to be warmed. It was as though Mabel herself was still lounging on a window seat, watching with great pleasure, the comings and goings, people coming back to life with wonder about their own mystery and that of others.

"The absence of sharp edges and corners, the diverse materials used, the small steps between rooms, produces the kind of empathy that welcomes and accepts all. There's an air of non-judgment that engages the creative spirit here, innocence returns and it feels easy to talk with people, natural to be curious. It's easy to accept all of yourself and others, which allows life to just happen and unfold without struggle of resistance."

Katrin's words reminded me of Carolynn Rafman's comment about everything unfolding so easily when she was up at Mabel's.

"When you enter Mabel's space," Katrin continued, "You feel

embraced and accepted. There's a feeling of wholeness, where inner wisdom, the sensory body and the intellect are grounded in one connected whole and this makes you feel you are home. Travelers from any walk of life feel welcome. There's a trust that whatever is expressed is gently folded and grounded and uplifted into the bigger mystery of life.

"Is it the Taos Mountain, is it the desert, is it Mabel?" she pondered. "It's hard to say, but one thing is for sure. Mabel intuitively founded a place where forces of destiny crossed to create an opening, a portal much like an acupuncture point. Once touched, it transforms and delivers you to the greater flow of Life and Mystery.

"After I completed the workshop," Katrin continued, "I'd learned to trust the process and feel comfortable just painting what came out of me, not to have to understand. If you allow pain to move, eventually it transforms into light. If you allow it to freeze, it stops life from moving.

"My time at Mabel's and the workshop helped me to understand why it's important for me to trust my intuition. Intuition appears to be the superhighway to allow the mysterious to unfold in my life. I had lost connection with someone for two years and after Mabel's, I felt love in a place where there had been anger, hurt and resentment. I felt my heart again, I could act, and my love was warmly received. I was able to feel free and joyful. My burdens lifted and that sense of presence helped others do the same.

"I changed the space of my home for a better energy flow so that it felt more like home, a place of joy and surprises, trust and safety that I like to come to and go from."

One of my last winters in Taos, I took a workshop at Mabel's on Native American dreaming. I recall sitting with a small group, in the classroom across the *acequia* from the Big House. As I savored the fragrance that filled the room: sweet sage and the pungence of *coupal*, made from resin, our group leader began to play a dreamy rhythm on his drum, and I could hear Phoebe Cottam describe the way Tony Luhan, after thanking the cook for "nice meal," would retreat to his room down the hall and play the drums softly.

Christmas Eve at the Pueblo

The last Christmas my husband, my daughter and I spent in Taos was especially magical. On December 23, they arrived on the shuttle from Albuquerque just as a gentle fluffy snow began to fall. We walked up the lane to Mabel's. The courtyard was deserted, the doves in their dovecotes. Lights gleamed in the windows.

On Christmas Eve, the Pueblo welcomes visitors. By the time we got there, the sunset was fading and the long road leading in was crowded either side with parked cars with license plates from all over. As we followed the crowds, the bell from the little church of San Geronimo began to ring. Behind the pyramid of mud houses, the snow-covered Sacred Mountain rose from the smoke of dozens of giant bonfires which blazed and crackled.

It was freezing cold and we'd been warned to dress in all our winter gear. The church bell continued to clang. After Vespers Mass, a group of warriors in traditional garb appeared from the doorway, carrying high a statue of the Virgin Mary beneath a cloth canopy. The procession included a group of young girls in white dresses who we hoped were wearing thermal underwear.

The bells continued to clang, the warriors fired their hunting rifles into the air and the crowd, pressed shoulder to shoulder, followed the procession around the plaza.

In spite of our down jackets, hats, scarves and gloves, it was bone chilling. Our eyes watered from cold and smoke but we were entranced by the spectacle, by the solemnity of the tradition, by the majesty of the setting. We wouldn't have missed it for anything.

Afterward we warmed ourselves at the Taos Inn, around the gorgeous Christmas tree. We drank hot cider and sang Christmas carols. The local vet sang a wonderful tenor *Silent Night*. Afterwards we walked, holding hands, through the falling snow to 220 Morada Lane. Somewhere out on the snow-covered Pueblo land beyond Mabel's, a pack of coyotes yipped and howled.

Santa Fe

In spite of missing each other, one of the gifts of our winters apart had been, for David and me, the opportunity to develop our writing, for during our separations, we each had time. We became, as Rilke advised, guardians of each other's "artistic solitude." We always looked forward to the weeks David flew in from Montreal, savoring each moment of our time.

After some years, David was able to spend more of each winter in New Mexico. My house on Morada Lane, though its tiny rooms were perfect for me, felt too cramped for two of us, and after twelve winters in Taos I was finally ready for a change.

We found our perfect place. The comfortable old house, just up the hill from the Santa Fe Plaza, was built, hacienda-style around an inner courtyard which filled every room in the house with light. There was plenty of room for our books. There was even a large, bright separate studio, perfect for teaching, and I began to give sessions based on my evolving work with houses.

Leaving Taos and my cozy little house on Morada Lane which had nurtured me for twelve winters, was however, a difficult decision. At first, each morning I thought of my strolls up the lane to Mabel's.

I wanted to connect my tie in Taos with Santa Fe and one of the first places I visited shortly after the move, was 1260 Canyon Road, where Phoebe Cottam had lived for the first twelve years of her life.

The old adobe homes of Phoebe's day, now house a mile of art galleries and boutiques interspersed with two high-end restaurants, cafés, a teahouse and a Tibetan center.

Phoebe's home was right at the end of what is now "Upper Canyon Road." Her childhood home is concealed behind high fences, on a ridge, with a fine view of valley and mountains. As I looked up at the house, I imagined her sneaking through the gate in the wall next door to Colonel Andy's, then being unable to get out.

Another day, as I walked down Palace Avenue by the former Sunmount Sanatorium. I thought of Mabel's arrival in Santa Fe in 1917, to meet her husband Maurice Sterne. Her son, John Evans, had appeared, looking excited and happy. He had a yellow silk handkerchief knotted around his neck and spurs on his boots. "This is a swell place, Mother!" he told me. "You'll love it!"

Later they went to visit artist, Paul Burlin, in Santa Fe for tea, where his Modernist paintings hung on the walls. His wife, Natalie Curtis, a talented musician, and musicologist, had gone west by herself, years before, been welcomed to study music with the Hopi, and spent time at First and Second Mesa listening to daily songs. She received permission from the Hopi to write down their traditional music. Later, she was accepted into many of the pueblos where she repeated the process. Her book, *The Indians: Authentic Native American Legends, Lore and Music,* was published in 1907.

Mabel described Natalie Curtis as "a little old doll that had been left out in the sun and rain." Also present at that tea was Alice Corbin Henderson, poet and co-editor of *Poetry Magazine*, whose daughter, "little Alice" would marry Mabel's son.

A year or so after we moved to Santa Fe, the house next door came up for sale. Each time I passed, I wished for a good friend to move in. Then one morning my wish was granted. Gayle Lux had just moved in. She was standing outside her front gate with an enormous female Harlequin Great Dane. As it turned out, we were the same age. Both of us spent the summers on the east coast.

We began to walk our dogs together. Quincy, her Dane, and

Caruso, my big white borzoi who had followed Bianca, greeted each other with barking and much tail waving. They always enjoyed each other's company and on one occasion soared right over the living room sofa as they chased each other.

Gayle was a physicist, and had been involved in cutting-edge work at Berkeley. One day, over blue corn burritos at The Shed, we were discussing the current status of women, specifically an article she had read about attitudes in Silicon Valley. How far had attitudes to women progressed since Mabel's time?

"You know," said Gayle, "I was working in an environment that was predominantly male, and there was still an unspoken feeling that as a woman you had to work harder to be accepted, to prove you were as good as your male colleagues."

It turned out that Gayle and I shared a Taos connection. One summer, she bought a small trailer and so enjoyed exploring the National Parks that she became interested in owning a campground. She contacted a broker who began to fly her around to look at prospective properties. A ten acre campground in Taos canyon caught her fancy and she decided to go ahead and buy it.

Though we'd both been in Taos in the early nineties, we'd never met as I'd spent my time there in winter, Gayle in summer. However, our Taos connection helped forge a bond which made my move from Taos to Santa Fe feel more coherent. I was delighted when I learned she'd become a docent at The Harwood Museum. This brought back pleasant memories of sitting in the Agnes Martin room with those big, spacious, horizontal paintings.

"I went back and forth between Berkeley and Taos," Gayle told me. "I liked the campground, the building where I lived had an upstairs, so I could be very private. I liked meeting people, Quincy loved everyone and they all loved her. I didn't actually spend much time in the town because there was so much to do out at the campground. I loved the land itself. It's so beautiful around Taos, especially the mountains."

Return to Taos

When I first went to Taos my knowledge of Buffalo, New York, was limited to what I read in Mabel's *Intimate Memories*. Then later, as David and I made our winter migrations between Montreal and New Mexico, we decided to take the road down through Buffalo then southwest around Lake Erie.

It was early winter and the sky was a leaden grey. My first impression as we drove down the highway that parallels Lake Erie, was of grey metal, of factories, some of them apparently closed, of old red-bricked neighborhoods which had seen better times, once stately old houses which must have once enjoyed an unobstructed lake view, now diminished by noise and the network of highways.

Later, I discovered that Mabel's childhood home, the solid brick mansion, square with a cupola on top, on the corner of North and Delaware, was no longer there, replaced by The Westbrook Apartments, a ten floor building that prides itself on its "fine city living" and a summer barbecue on a roof-top with an impressive view of city buildings and the lake.

The old mansions of "Millionaires Row" now house part of the University of Buffalo with much of the space now filled with the inevitable parking lots. The nearby house where her little friend, Nina Wilcox lived is, however, a historically preserved site. When President William McKinley visited Buffalo for the Pan American Exposition in 1901, he was assassinated. President Theodore Roosevelt was sworn in at the house of Ansley Wilcox, Nina's father. The Inaugural National Historic site, open to visitors, remains a columned mansion.

Trinity Church, built in 1869, ten years before Mabel's birth and the Forest Lawn Cemetery remain. I did my best to picture young Mabel and her friends clipping along Delaware and around the cemetery park in the two-seated cart pulled by their pony, Cupid, but try as I might, I was unable to recreate anything lighthearted.

The golden era of Buffalo with its steel and banking barons has passed. Recently, new life has been breathed into the city. The waterfront has been revitalized, there are tours of Frank Lloyd Wright Houses, Frederick Olmsted parks, fine museums. In May, 2017, the Burchfield Penney Art Center hosted the exhibit, *Mabel Dodge Luhan and Company: American Moderns and the West*.

For me, however, Buffalo is too strongly associated with the images in Mabel's *Intimate Memories*, of the constrictions of her loveless childhood home on Delaware, of her unfortunate first marriage and her sad response to the birth of her son.

Though she claimed that she wouldn't have had the city of her birth any other way, as we drove past the icy shore of Lake Erie and left that winter city behind, I couldn't wait to reach that sun-drenched world which opened at the top of Morada Lane.

Few places escape change and fifteen years after I'd left my cozy little house at 220 Morada Lane, as I contemplate a visit to Taos I am apprehensive.

My heart lifts as I emerge from the Rio Grande Gorge and approach the final stretch of the road to Taos. At the top of the last hill, I round the bend and suddenly the valley lies before me luminous in late morning sunshine. The dark snake of the Rio Grande twists to the left, and ahead rise the snow-tipped mountains, all the way to Colorado. She's up there, straight ahead, my mountain.

In the valley, the soft nestle of adobes has expanded in the decades since I first crept from the Gorge in that long ago blizzard. I recall the first time I saw the valley below me in the sunshine and felt as though I were discovering Shangri La. Then the road curves down and up again and the second vista reveals itself. Now it's straight ahead through the sage plains. I roll my windows down to inhale deeply that Taos smell of *piñon* smoke, cedar and sage.

We're just four miles from Taos. Bianca and Aslan are now a pair of cloud borzoi in the sky; my new big white borzoi companion, Caruso, stands gazing attentively through the window. We slow down through the messy little town of Ranchos de Taos with its woodpiles and bales of straw and consignment furniture, with the flat-backed church made famous by Georgia O'Keeffe and there on the left is the once infamous Old Martina's bar and dance hall, now transformed into an upscale restaurant.

We pass the Chevron gas station where I learned how to fill my car's gas tank, past the car wash with the long hose that practically knocked me off my feet when I turned it on in February of 1991.

And now we're on the home run. My faithful old Explorer and Caruso and Oliver Wu, the Pekinese and Rupert the pug. We pass The Sagebrush Inn where David and I went one Christmas to learn the two-step, past the Singer Sewing Machine store where I bought a used vacuum cleaner necessary to control the fine film of ceiling dust at 220 Morada Lane. Coming up to the old, once walled town, we pass The Spotted Bear on the right, the wooden railings still draped with velvet and lace skirts and tops, a stronghold of hippie finery.

There's the Plaza on the left. The End of the Universe Café, where I took tea with Sal and Peanut, has disappeared. The Taos Inn on the right looks the same as always and Bent Street feels unchanged. The John Dunn Plaza, where I set off to find a notebook that late summer morning, and ended up with a notebook and a house, has changed little, with its leather boutique and fabric store that sells silks and brocades in rich rainbow hues.

We park outside the Bent Street Deli. As usual, the server tells me "watch your step" as I follow her out to the covered patio where heaters whirr overhead. I order a bowl of pueblo stew, which turns out to be corn and beans and squash with green chili, served with pumpernickel. I watch the handful of tourists. Today's warm for winter, fifty-one degrees, with that antique lavender Taos sky.

I visit Susan-next door. She has sold Susan Wilder Fine Art to her partner. The three borzoi we visited the day Bianca stole the filet mignon straight from the grill, have joined Bianca in the clouds. Her new companion, Chip, is a handsome fellow with a silken coat of silvery grey.

Finally I drive up Morada Lane. The mud has been replaced by paving, the tumbledown shack at the end of the lane is now a solid two-story adobe with plenty of character. At 220, I push open the tall *latilla* gate, apprehensive, because I no longer own the little house. The new owner has removed the old wraparound greenhouse and its beds of hardy red geraniums. I wonder what he did with them. Instead, there's a wide wooden deck, which actually looks good and would be great for summer entertaining . The house looks longer and leaner without the greenhouse. I remember how Susanna described it as "funky."

I take one last look at the house, then close the gate behind me. Back at the car, I water and walk the dogs, reload them and drive up the hill to the parking lot at Mabel's. I climb the wooden steps and cross the small wooden bridge which spans the dry *acequia*. I imagine Mabel's guests daydreaming in the wooden gliders. The dovecotes are empty. Where are the pigeons?

Across the uneven cobblestones of the courtyard, to the front door with its sea green, red and white design and into the living room with the old wooden floor, and worn Mosad Persian rug. The furniture is comfortable and there are good smells drifting from the kitchen. Maria is not in today. When I walk to the edge of the pueblo land, there is a new fence with a gate in it. There she is, my mountain. I stand and look at her and am grateful for those twelve healing years.

A tall man in tattered jeans and dreads is reading by the door at Caffé Tazza. A white-haired woman in a perky red hat and long floral skirt has taken a table in a patch of sunshine by the window that overlooks a patio of winter-wilted white hollyhocks.

I take my latte into the big room. Just outside the window a shaggy black mutt is sunning himself and a woman clad in the requisite layers of woolen clothing carries a well-bundled baby across the patio.

A woman and a man with a grey ponytail are sitting at the big table by the piano working on the budget for a forthcoming event. Two rough-haired men with newspapers are talking about a new play one of them is working to complete. One has a tiny Yorkie on the bench beside him. It's warm and sunny in here. The front page of *The New Mexican* reads, *Santa Fe Realty Agent Held at Gunpoint.*

Mabel's Grave

"We have the prettiest graveyards in the world here in this valley, I believe," wrote Mabel, "all sown with pale blue or white wooden crosses, where the wreaths of pink and red and orange paper hang since All Souls' Day, and have been wetted by snow and blanched by the sun, until they are mellowed and melted into a dream-like impressionistic picture of their first hard, crisp contours. There is a small, rakish, turquoise blue cross planted out there with the letters, M.D. painted on it, that Bobby used to swear marks my grave; reflecting, I suppose, the belief of that time that I was buried here!"[72]

On Dragoon Lane, I pass the row of small adobe cottages with their blue and turquoise wooden trim. A woman in a lilac parka and blue pants holds a ginger cat beside a rusted car. At the end, just past number 121, a metal arch holds the sign, Kit Carson Memorial Park. A path curves through family grave plots surrounded by low metal fences. Brilliantly colored plastic flowers have replaced the ones I remember from my winters on Morada Lane, which were made of the faded tissue paper Mabel described.

A white-haired woman walks slowly along the path in the adjacent park where the ice-skating rink played music all those winters. A long-tailed magpie lights on the fence.

In the corner closest to the fence is Mabel's grave. A simple slab and stone marker 18 inches high with, simply, Mabel Dodge Luhan, Feb

26, 1879 – Aug 13, 1962. That's all. Beside her is the marker for her old friend and painter, Ralph Meyers.

At our Taos Inn lunch, Phoebe Cottam had told me, "There was no room left in the cemetery. Meyers told Mabel she could be buried on top of him, he already had a reserved place. And so she is."

On the ground in front of her grave is a baked apple with a few bites taken out. There's another on the stone. A row of pennies, an empty sample bottle of Jack Daniels whiskey, a fat white candle in a glass holder, an empty can of Squirt soft drink, a circle of red cloth, a peace sign and a Celestial Seasonings chamomile tea bag.

The branches of the nearby tree are bare and birds twitter. It's all very peaceful. What would Mabel think?

The day I finally left 220 Morada Lane for good, it was beginning to snow. Through a wintery sunlight you could see the shining snowflakes. I parked my car at the lookout where twelve winters earlier the fierce blizzard had blotted out that first breathtaking view of the Rio Grande. In the valley below, Taos town, with its outlying sprawl, nestled at the foot of the sacred mountain. I engraved the scene in my mind.

When I was nine years old I won a copy of George MacDonald's classic, *The Princess and the Goblin*. Princess Irene climbs the stairs in the castle where she lives, becomes lost and discovers a room in the tower where a beautiful lady with long silver hair is seated at a spinning wheel. She tells the child that she is spinning a ball of protection for her granddaughter. When she leaves, Princess Irene takes with her the ball of shining material which will protect her and always lead her safely back to her grandmother. Now, when I think of Taos, it hovers in that shimmering light, a high, strange unchanging realm at the foot of my magic mountain, whose protection feels timeless.

Epilogue

Twenty five years after we met that winter day at The Taos Book Shop, my friend Susanna visits me in Santa Fe. On a glorious sunny day in October we drive up to Taos. We pass roadside stands of apples, pumpkins and *ristras*, those long, hanging bunches of red chili peppers. We pass the bend where the Rio Grande becomes a stretch of churning whitewater, then climb into the Sangre de Christos.

At the first lookout we slow down and there in the valley below nestles Taos, its borders gradually seeping outwards with new developments.

The traffic on Pueblo del Norte is still bumper to bumper. As we creep by The Taos Inn I think fondly of lunch with my friend Susan and Phoebe Cottam.

We drive out to Blueberry Hill. Susanna's house has a new wing added onto her kitchen and there are more houses out there with that spectacular view of the mountain.

We park outside Caffé Tazza. "Two women from Dixon just bought it," the girl at the reception tells us. "They're planning to do some renovation." The big room is empty but the geraniums look healthy. The Taos Book Shop is now Parson's Gallery. The sign still warns, *Watch Your Head*. Susanna recalls the day John Nichols came in and bumped his head hard on the beam.

The woman at the desk is friendly. The art is classic Taos and the southwest. Sunsets, quaint adobe cottages with blue and turquoise doors, the mountain, the pueblo, those scenes which had lured artists to Mabel's almost a hundred years ago. We wander slowly through the small rooms.

"Sometimes Barbara and I would play Spanish music and dance here in the big room," Susanna tells me. "We had a lot of fun."

Finally we head along Kit Carson and up Morada Lane to Mabel's. The parking lot below the building where the workshops are held is full, so we drive to the top of the lane and park near the Pueblo land. The fence has been repaired and there's a new gate. Out there on the sage plain the white cross still stands.

The living room at Mabel's is deserted. The woman in the small office, Carol, is friendly. Maria is no longer working at Mabel's. "But her daughter, Vanessa, is in the kitchen," Carol tells us.

One hundred years after Mabel arrived in Taos, her undaunted spirit, which refused to accept anything less than authenticity, lives on in the workshops and retreats offered in 2017: *Sense of Place; A Muse in Winter; Creativity Rediscovered; Spirit Messengers.*

We linger over our lunch in Doc Martin's Restaurant at The Taos Inn where things feel the way they always did. I'm delighted that we've been seated at the table for two tucked down a few steps with a view of the patio, the table where Phoebe Cottam shared her memories of Mabel. I can still hear her chuckle as she tells me about baby John becoming rambunctious on Mabel's lap and recall Brett's admonishments against slipping the baby sips of bourbon.

After lunch we stroll across the road to Bent Street. Susanna is browsing the Kitchen Shop on Bent Street for gifts. I'm leaning against the adobe wall soaking up afternoon sunshine. A woman comes up to me. Her silver-grey hair is tied in a ponytail. A notebook bulges from her purse. "I wonder if you could help me," she says. "I just took the bus up from Santa Fe and I'm looking for the Mabel Dodge House."

Bibliography

Brett, Dorothy. *Lawrence and Brett. A Friendship.* Santa Fe: Sunstone Press, 2006. Original edition: New York: J. B. Lippincott Company, 1933.

Dewitt, Miriam Hapgood. *Taos: A Memory.* Albuquerque: University of New Mexico Press, 1992.

Luhan, Mabel Dodge. *Intimate Memories: Background, Volume One.* Santa Fe: Sunstone Press, 2015. Original Edition, New York: Harcourt, Brace and Company, 1933.

———. *Intimate Memories: European Experiences, Volume Two.* Santa Fe: Sunstone Press, 2015. Original Edition, Harcourt, Brace and Company, 1935

———. *Intimate Memories: Movers and Shakers, Volume Three.* Santa Fe, Sunstone Press, 2019. Original Edition, New York: Harcourt, Brace and Company, 1936.

———. *Intimate Memories: Edge of Taos Desert, An Escape to Reality, Volume Four.* Santa Fe: Sunstone Press, 2019. Original Edition, New York: Harcourt, Brace and Company, 1937.

———. *Lorenzo in Taos*. Santa Fe: Sunstone Press, 2007. Original Edition, New York: Alfred Knopf, 1932.

———. *Winter in Taos*. Santa Fe: Sunstone Press, 2007. Original Edition, New York: Harcourt, Brace and Company, 1935.

Poling-Kempes, Lesley. *Ladies of the Canyons*. Tucson: University of Arizona Press, 2015.

Rudnick, Lois Palken. *New Woman, New Worlds*. Albuquerque: University of New Mexico Press, 1984

———. *Utopian Vistas*. Albuquerque: University of New Mexico Press, 1996.

———. *The Suppressed Memoirs of Mabel Dodge Luhan*. Albuquerque: University of New Mexico Press, 2012.

Notes

1. Mabel Dodge Luhan, *Edge of Taos Desert*, p. 3
2. Ibid., p. 6
3. Mabel Dodge Luhan, *Intimate Memories; Movers and Shakers*, p. 111
4. Ibid., p. 179
5. Ibid., p. 142
6. Ibid., p. 145
7. Mabel Dodge Luhan, *Movers and Shakers*
8. Mabel Dodge Luhan, *Winter in Taos*
9. Mabel Dodge Luhan, *Intimate Memories: Background*, p. 7-8
10. Ibid., p. 32
11. Ibid., p. 41
12. Mabel Dodge Luhan, *Intimate Memories: European Experiences*, p. 53
13. Ibid., p. 55
14. Ibid., p. 59
15. Ibid., p. 74
16. Ibid., p. 77
17. Ibid., p. 80
18. Ibid., p. 102
19. Mabel Dodge Luhan, *Intimate Memories: Movers and Shakers*, p. 112
20. Ibid., p. 112
21. Lois Palken Rudnick, *Mabel Dodge Luhan: New Woman, New Worlds*.
22. Ibid., p. 94

23. Mabel Dodge Luhan, *Intimate Memories: Movers and Shakers.*
24. Ibid., p. 145
25. Ibid.p. 149
26. Ibid.p. 182
27. Mabel Dodge Luhan, *Edge of Taos Desert*, p. 148
28. Mabel Dodge Luhan, *Winter in Taos*
29. Mabel Dodge Luhan, *Edge of Taos Desert*, p. 58
30. Mabel Dodge Luhan, *Winter in Taos*
31. Ibid., p. 63
32. Ibid.p. 33
33. Ibid.
34. Mabel Dodge Luhan, *Lorenzo in Taos*
35. Ibid.
36. Miriam Hapgood Dewitt, *Taos: A Memory*
37. Ibid.
38. Mabel Dodge Luhan, *Lorenzo in Taos*
39. Ibid.
40. Ibid.
41. Ibid.
42. Ibid.
43. Ibid.
44. Ibid
45. Ibid.
46. Dorothy Brett, *Lawrence and Brett: A Friendship*
47. Ibid.
48. Ibid.
49. Mabel Dodge Luhan, *Winter in Taos*
50. Lois Palken Rudnick, *Mabel Dodge Luhan: New Woman, New Worlds*, p. 95
51. Mabel Dodge Luhan, *Intimate Memories: Movers and Shakers*, p. 124
52. Mabel Dodge Luhan, *Winter in Taos*
53. Ibid.
54. Lois Palken Rudnick, *The Suppressed Memories of Mabel Dodge Luhan,* p. 158
55. Ibid., p. 165
56. Ibid.
57. Mabel Dodge Luhan, *Intimate Memories: Background,* p. 6

58. Mabel Dodge Luhan, *Intimate Memories: European Experiences*
59. Ibid., p. 79
60. Ibid., p. 75
61. Ibid., p. 169
62. Mabel Dodge Luhan, *Intimate Memories: Movers and Shakers*, p. 145
63. Mabel Dodge Luhan, *Intimate Memories: Background*.
64. Mabel Dodge Luhan, *Intimate Memories: European Experiences*.
65. Mabel Dodge Luhan, *Intimate Memories: European Experiences*, p. 67
66. Mabel Dodge Luhan, *Intimate Memories: Background*, p. 50
67. Mabel Dodge Luhan, *Winter in Taos*
68. Mabel Dodge Luhan, *Winter in Taos*
69. Ibid.
70. Ibid.
71. Ibid.
72. Ibid.

www.ingramcontent.com/pod-product-compliance
Lightning Source LLC
Chambersburg PA
CBHW021914180426
43198CB00035B/565